T0271346

Proposal Writing for Business Research Projects

This book helps students with the initial phases of their business research project, offering a clear step-by-step approach from defining aims and research questions through to conducting literature reviews and writing a methodology.

Features to aid learning include chapter objectives, plentiful real-life examples to demonstrate good practice, exercises to apply the concepts and further reading for proactive investigation.

A self-contained guide to every stage of writing an effective business research proposal, this text should be recommended reading for all advanced undergraduate and postgraduate students studying Business Research Methods and embarking on a research project of their own.

Dr Peter Samuels graduated with a first class honours in mathematics from Cambridge University and a PhD in mathematics and cognitive psychology from the University of Reading. He currently works as Senior Lecturer in Research Practice in the Business School of Birmingham City University. He leads undergraduate and master's level dissertation modules with about 1,000 students per year. He is passionate about developing both staff and students into competent academics and researchers. He is a self-taught academic writing tutor and previously set up and led a statistics advisory service at his university. He is involved in project and voluntary work in East Africa where he trains doctoral students in research proposal writing and research methods. He has published widely in mathematics education, research methods and learning development.

Routledge Focus on Business and Management

The fields of business and management have grown exponentially as areas of research and education. This growth presents challenges for readers trying to keep up with the latest important insights. *Routledge Focus on Business and Management* presents small books on big topics and how they intersect with the world of business research.

Individually, each title in the series provides coverage of a key academic topic, whilst collectively, the series forms a comprehensive collection across the business disciplines.

Neuroscience and Entrepreneurship Research
Researching Brain-Driven Entrepreneurship
Víctor Pérez Centeno

Proposal Writing for Business Research Projects
Peter Samuels

Systems Thinking and Sustainable Healthcare Delivery
Ben Fong

Gender Diversity and Inclusion at Work
Divergent Views from Turkey
Zeynep Özsoy, Mustafa Şenyücel and Beyza Oba

Management and Visualisation
Seeing Beyond the Strategic
Gordon Fletcher

For more information about this series, please visit: www.routledge.com/ Routledge-Focus-on-Business-and-Management/book-series/FBM

Proposal Writing for Business Research Projects

Peter Samuels

Routledge
Taylor & Francis Group
LONDON AND NEW YORK

First published 2023
by Routledge
4 Park Square, Milton Park, Abingdon, Oxon OX14 4RN

and by Routledge
605 Third Avenue, New York, NY 10158

Routledge is an imprint of the Taylor & Francis Group, an informa business

© 2023 Peter Samuels

The right of Peter Samuels to be identified as author of this work has been asserted in accordance with sections 77 and 78 of the Copyright, Designs and Patents Act 1988.

British Library Cataloguing-in-Publication Data
A catalogue record for this book is available from the British Library

ISBN: 978-1-032-22721-4 (hbk)
ISBN: 978-1-032-25812-6 (pbk)
ISBN: 978-1-003-28513-7 (ebk)

DOI: 10.4324/9781003285137

Typeset in Times New Roman
by Apex CoVantage, LLC

Contents

Preface

Why this book?

Hello. My name is Dr Peter Samuels and I work for Birmingham City University. Taylor & Francis asked me to write this book because they had seen some of my online resources (such as Samuels, 2017), and thought I might be able to write a book to help business students undertaking dissertations.

As far as we are aware, this is the first book on research proposal writing specifically for business students. Proposal writing is the important initial phase in doing a dissertation project. It combines many aspects of the whole dissertation process. We believe this specialist book on proposal writing in the context of doing a business dissertation project will be a useful resource to many students.

A bear eating fish

The main message of this book is the importance of **putting the reader first**. I like to think of writing proposals like a bear eating a fish as shown in Figure 0.1.

The fish represents your proposal. The bear represents your target reader – the proposal reviewer. You can see that this bear has too many fish to eat so it will focus on eating the high-protein parts. In the same way, proposal reviewers are busy people and probably have many proposals to read in a short period of time. Therefore, they will be looking for certain essential elements in your proposal, which you can think of as the high-protein parts. By following the principles explained in this book you will be able to give them a good taste.

Who is this book written for?

This book is written for final-year undergraduate and master's business students undertaking a dissertation. It might also be relevant to doctoral students, especially those for whom English is an additional language. The

Figure 0.1 Bear eating fish

content is also largely relevant to social science dissertations, although the examples are all taken from the business context.

What is unique about this book?

Apart from the title, this book uses actual business students' examples of writing.

It also emphasises academic writing development within the proposal writing process.

There are also some appendices at the end which address the next steps in the dissertation supervision process.

Who is the author?

I am Senior Lecturer in Research Practice. I work in the Business School at Birmingham City University. I have been teaching dissertation writing for over ten years. I am responsible for teaching and coordinating the supervision of over 800 undergraduate and master's dissertations students every year. I am also involved in voluntary work in East Africa where I teach intensive courses on proposal writing to doctoral students.

Acknowledgements

I would sincerely like to thank four dissertation students from Birmingham City University who allowed me to use their proposals as examples in this book. Their first names are Kate, Mollie, Tappasiya and Thomas. Each of them was awarded a distinction grade for their proposal but their work was not perfect. They therefore provide useful examples for learning purposes.

I would also like to thank my colleague Andrew Hambler for being my critical friend in the writing of this book.

Reference

Samuels, P. C. (2017) How to write a PhD proposal. Technical report. *ResearchGate*. Available at: www.researchgate.net/publication/322077097_How_to_Write_a_PhD_Proposal.

Introduction

Context

This book assumes that you are undertaking a research project in the academic subject of business as part of your undergraduate or master's degree. Business includes areas such as business management, human resource management, leadership, supply chain management, business information systems, entrepreneurship, marketing, economics, finance and accounting.

What is a proposal?

A proposal is a **statement of what you intend to do**. Proposals are commonly required in many areas of research as they encourage the researcher to **think about, decide** on and **articulate** what exactly they are planning to do. This provides an excellent opportunity for them to **receive feedback** at the formative stage of their research which can **improve their performance** and **reduce the risk of them going in the wrong direction**.

Why write a proposal?

Most undergraduate and master's level students are required to write a proposal for their dissertation projects. This comes at the start of their projects. It is likely to form part of their dissertation assessment with its own assignment brief and marking scheme. However, **this is not the main real reason for writing a proposal**.

The real **purpose** of a proposal is to **persuade the academic staff responsible for reviewing proposals** that you have **chosen a viable research project** in a **context** which you **understand,** and that you have a **credible plan** to carry it out.

Proposal reviewers are busy people (remember the bear and the fish metaphor from the preface). **They will not be impressed by long words, long**

DOI: 10.4324/9781003285137-1

sentences, a long document, or complex ideas. Instead, they are looking for interesting ideas and to be persuaded by a **clear and concise argument** that is correctly structured.

What makes a good proposal?

The first and most important aspect of a good proposal is to **choose a good topic**. This means that it should be **within the scope of your course**, of **interest** and **importance** to some group of people and **narrowly focused** so that it is **original** and **achievable**.

Secondly, your argument for choosing your topic (known as your **rationale**) needs to be **clear** and **persuasive**.

Thirdly, you need to demonstrate that you **understand the context** of your chosen topic in your background and literature review.

Fourthly, you need to have a **credible and persuasive plan** for collecting and analysing your data (your **method**), the theoretical context of this plan (your **methodology**) and its practical outworking over the time available (your **schedule**).

Finally, your proposal needs to be **well written and presented** and follow **the correct academic writing conventions**.

Added benefits

Proposal writing is the first phase on the dissertation journey and the first subject for discussion with your supervisor. It therefore acts as a gateway into your research experience.

Learning how to write a good proposal can help you to become a better academic writer. I do voluntary work helping doctoral students in other countries understand these principles because I have seen that this can change their lives and open doors for them.

Types of dissertation

All dissertations involve the **systematic collection and analysis of data**. However, in some places in this book, it is important to understand the differences between three main types of dissertation. These are distinguished by the **type of data that is being collected** and **how it is being analysed**, as shown in Table 0.1.

The three main types of dissertation are:

1   The **normal primary research dissertation** involves the researcher **collecting and analysing some data themselves,** for example by carrying out a questionnaire or interviews.

Table 0.1 Types of dissertation

		Collected data	
		Primary (you)	Secondary (others)
Analysis	Primary (you) Secondary (others)	1. Normal primary research dissertation	2. Secondary data primary analysis dissertation 3. Systematic review

2   The **secondary data primary analysis dissertation** involves the researcher **analysing a data set that someone else has already collected**. This could be data on the financial performance of organisations or some form of textual data already available in the public domain, such as customer comments on a product, advertising on social media or company reports. However, this does not include published journal articles.

3   The **systematic review dissertation** involves the researcher carrying out a **systematic secondary analysis of data which was collected, analysed and published by other researchers**. The main kind of data used is **published journal articles**.

Both the normal primary research dissertation and the secondary data primary analysis dissertation involve carrying out a literature review before the data is collected and analysed. This kind of review is known as a **narrative review** as it does not follow a systematic method.

However, in the systematic review dissertation, the literature review replaces the systematic collection and analysis of other kinds of data. This means that the review should follow a prescribed method, known as a **protocol**. The topic of a systematic review style dissertation is usually **broader in scope** than for the other two kinds of dissertation. For a recent publication on business systematic reviews, please see (Paul et al., 2021).

It is also useful at this stage to explain three common terms relating to **types of research**:

*   **Quantitative research** refers to the collection and analysis of **measurable quantities**, such as numbers and frequencies
*   **Qualitative research** refers to the collection and evaluation or interpretation of data which is often in **open textual** form
*   **Mixed methods research** refers to a combination of qualitative and quantitative research

Outline of the rest of this book

The rest of this book is divided into four parts:

Part 1: Selection and presenting your topic

The first part covers the topic selection and presentation process. Chapter 1 is about how to select a topic. Chapter 2 explains how to present your topic in what is known as its **front matter**.

Part 2: Academic writing

The second part covers some of the principles of academic writing. The different competencies involved in academic writing can be viewed as a tree, as shown in Figure I.1.

The competencies below the red dotted line are to do with writing general English rather than academic English (known as **functional skills**). For more information on these please refer to Bailey (2018) and Gillett (2021). All the other competencies are covered in this part except for document genre (as proposals are a type of document genre).

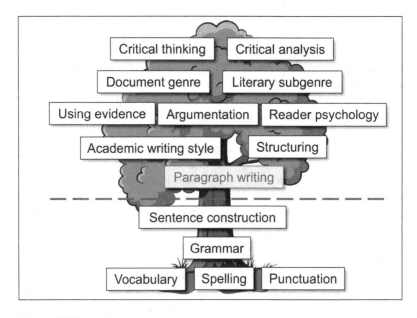

Figure I.1 The academic writing tree

Chapter 3 explains how to structure your proposal. Chapter 4 introduces basic aspects of academic writing style. Chapter 5 covers issues of academic integrity, including the correct use of evidence and avoiding plagiarism. Chapter 6 explains the principles of paragraph writing. Chapter 7 Introduces the two main argumentation styles and how to plan your argument.

Part 3: Writing your proposal

The third part of this book is about how to write the other essential parts of your proposal.

Chapter 8 covers writing the other parts of the introduction, including the background and the problem statement. Chapter 9 goes into depth on researching and writing a proposal literature review. Chapter 10 introduces conceptual frameworks. Chapter 11 explains how to write a methodology/method section. Chapter 12 is about writing a project plan and Chapter 13 covers how to cite and reference correctly.

Part 4: Beyond your proposal

The fourth part of this book provides advice on the next steps after you submit your proposal.

Chapter 14 covers time and stress management. Chapter 15 explains how to get the most out of your supervisory relationships and Chapter 16 introduces the next tasks to focus on after you submit your proposal.

References

Bailey, S. (2018) *Academic writing: A handbook for international students*. 5th edn. Abingdon: Routledge.

Gillett, A. (2021) *Using English for academic purposes for students in higher education: Academic writing*. Available at: www.uefap.com/writing/writfram.htm.

Paul, J., Merchant, A., Dwivedi, Y. K. and Rose, G. (2021) Writing an impactful review article: What do we know and what do we need to know? *Journal of Business Research*, 133, pp. 337–340. https://doi.org/10.1016/j.jbusres.2021.05.005.

Part One

Selecting and presenting your topic

1 Selecting your topic

Introduction

Coming up with a good topic idea is one of the hardest parts of the proposal writing process and maybe also the most important. The education system in most countries is focused on developing convergent thinking. However, topic selection involves creativity which includes divergent thinking. Selecting a good topic also involves reading, evaluating and identifying a viable data source as shown in Figure 1.1.

We shall explore these aspects in turn in the rest of this chapter.

The creative process

As mentioned above, the creative process involves both divergent and convergent thinking. It is the divergent aspect which many students find disturbing. Creative breakthroughs often come unexpectedly. After making a breakthrough there is still often a validation stage to confirm that the idea can work.

The most widely accepted model of the creative process was proposed by Henri Poincaré (1908). It has four stages:

- **Preparation** – conscious work on a problem
- **Incubation** – unconscious work
- **Illumination** – a sudden insight (known as a gestalt)
- **Verification** – a second phase of conscious work to shape the insight

The preparation stage

For topic selection, the **preparation stage** involves identifying the scope of possible dissertation topics and some key concepts or areas of interest. These concepts or areas can lead to identifying keywords which can be entered into **Google Scholar** (https://scholar.google.co.uk/) as search terms.

DOI: 10.4324/9781003285137-3

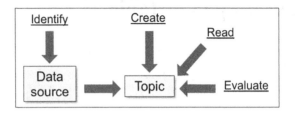

Figure 1.1 The topic selection process

Source: (Samuels, 2021)

Figure 1.2 Output from the first Google Scholar search

Source: (Google, 2022a)

Google Scholar is a really useful tool to use at this stage. Later on in literature search we recommend using the front search engine from your university library or specific databases. Google Scholar prioritises the sources with the best match and also those considered to be the most important academically as measured by the **citation rate** (the number of citations obtained per year).

Example

A master's student is interested in the implementation of new information and communication technology (ICT) systems in small and medium-sized enterprises (SMEs) in the Nigerian retail sector. This could lead to a Google Scholar search using the following keywords, *ict, retail, sme* and *nigeria,* giving the result shown in Figure 1.2.

There are about 9,700 matching articles (or hits). The first hit has received 96 citations since 2011 (i.e. in 11 years). The second hit has received 25 citations since 2013. The third hit has 25 citations over five years. So the citation rate of the first article is the highest. All three articles are available as PDFs but the first and the second ones may require creating a ResearchGate account before you can access them. ResearchGate (www.researchgate. net/) is an academic social networking site. The articles are about different aspects of ICT adoption by SMEs in Nigeria. None of these three articles seem to mention the retail sector.

In order to emphasise the need to identify articles specifically concerning retail, a second search was undertaken with the following search terms: *ict*, "*retail sector*", *sme*, and *nigeria*. Putting quotation marks around the phrase *retail sector* limits the search to articles which match this whole phrase. The results of the search are shown in Figure 1.3.

This second search returned with over 2,500 hits. This first hit seems to be a good match. It has a good citation rate, was published in the last ten years, and is available as a PDF. It would therefore seem to be a good article for the student to download and read. The subject is a particular kind of ICT system (e-commerce) and seems to be limited to small retail businesses rather than medium-sized ones. However, it would require further reading to know exactly what definition is being used and how relevant it is to the student's initial idea.

The goal at this stage is not to be systematic in the literature searching, but rather to find some relevant research articles to establish what has already been studied and what is already known in the field. Clearly, the

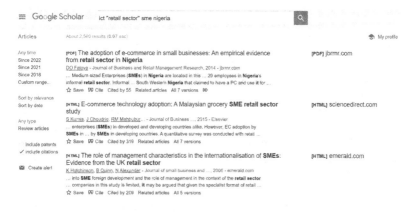

Figure 1.3 Output from the second Google Scholar search

Source: (Google, 2022b)

scope of the student's proposed research is currently too broad to be unique as there already appears to be articles published on this subject.

The preparation phase ends with obtaining a few relevant research articles and reading the most relevant parts of them. The goal of the next two stages is for the student to identify a unique topic that they can realistically investigate.

The incubation and illumination stages

The **incubation stage** is hard to explain in detail as it involves the subconscious. The best time for this is when you are asleep or relaxing, thinking about something completely different. Talking through your ideas with other people, writing down your reflections, or doing something recreational with a low verbal content (such as playing sport, cooking, listening to music, playing an instrument, or doing some physical exercise) might also help stimulate this process.

The outcome of this process is the **illumination stage**. This is where your preparation such as reading, understanding the need to be focused and original and your practical opportunities to collect data causes an idea to come to mind.

The importance of data

The other part of Figure 1.1 we have not yet covered is the identification of a data source. This is critical for selecting a good topic. Dissertations are essentially about **identifying, obtaining and systematically analysing data**.

Example

Following on from the previous example, the supervisor asked the master's student why she was interested in the implementation of ICT systems in Nigerian retail SMEs. She replied that it was because of her family business and the examples of good practice she had seen in UK retail SMEs, and she was wondering what might be applicable in Nigeria. This enabled the supervisor to identify one source of data – the family business in Nigeria, which could be framed as a **case study**. Another possible source of data would be the retail SMEs in the UK that the student admired, but these might require a different form of data collection.

This helps to narrow down the student's topic onto one specific retail SME in Nigeria along with a comparison with retail SMEs in the UK.

Other topic selection strategies

Horn (2012: 12–17) suggests some other topic selection strategies:

- **Career goals** – if you know what career you want to get into after you graduate, this strategy involves making contacts with people already working in this area. It could take the form of finding out more about what they do or how the managed to end up in their roles. Your dissertation then becomes a vehicle for building a network and promoting your interest in working in this field. This can be particularly useful in the creative industries where many opportunities arise through relational networking rather than traditional job advertising.
- **Solving a practical problem** – if you already have a part-time job, or you are closely associated with a business, you may have identified something which could be improved in the way this business operates. This strategy means using your dissertation to precisely define what the issue is that needs to be improved then designing a solution. You might also implement and evaluate a solution; this is known as **action research**. However, when you present your topic in your proposal (see Chapter 8) it should be in the form of a problem that needs to be solved, not a solution you have already come up with.
- **Tutor-driven** – if you are allowed to suggest or choose your own supervisor, you might have access to their research profile. Looking at what they have already published could be the basis for selecting a topic which might be of interest to them and hence improve your chances of a good supervision relationship.

Qualities of a good topic

Here are some qualities of a good topic (see also Horn, 2012: 19):

- It **relates to theory** (a theory is **a recognised system of related concepts which explain how something works in a general sense**) – you should not choose a topic that is entirely practical; you need to be able to theorise what you are planning to do in some way.
- It can be **defined concisely** – see Chapter 2.
- It is a **business topic**, so it needs to relate to individuals, groups or organisations and your potential findings should be **relevant** to (some of) them.
- It should be **achievable** within the timeframe available.
- It should be **easy to access the data** – see above.

- It should comply with your university's regulations (such as ethical and safe data collection).
- It should have some **element of originality** – this is often achieved through unique data being analysed. You should also search the literature to ensure that you are not replicating someone else's work exactly.
- Finally, you should personally find it **interesting** – this is very important later in the research process as interesting topics foster **intrinsic motivation** which can help you to have **finishing energy**.

Evaluating whether your topic idea has these qualities aligns with the **verification** stage of the creative process introduced above.

A final word

Topic selection often feels like a somewhat random, chaotic or haphazard process. This can be disturbing if you are used to being told what to do, especially as it comes at the start of your research project. It is important to do this well because **the overall success of your project often depends directly on the quality of your chosen topic**.

Often your first idea will not work. It is important to be patient and give time and space for your subconscious to work. If you realise that you have to change your initial idea, try to **modify** it rather than starting over again from scratch.

References

Google (2022a) *Output from Google Scholar UK with search terms ict retail sme nigeria*. Available at: https://scholar.google.co.uk/scholar?hl=en&as_sdt=0%2C5&q=ict+retail+sme+nigeria&btnG=.

Google (2022b) *Output from Google Scholar UK with search terms ict "retail sector" sme nigeria*. Available at: https://scholar.google.co.uk/scholar?hl=en&as_sdt=0%2C5&q=ict+%22retail+sector%22+sme+nigeria&btnG=.

Horn, R. (2012) *Researching and writing dissertations: A complete guide for business and management students*. 2nd edn. London: CIPD.

Poincaré, H. (1908) L'invention mathématique. *Bulletin de l'Institut Général de Psychologie*, 8e année(3), pp. 175–196.

Samuels, P. C. (2021) Dissertations in 20 steps – a platonic discussion. Technical report. *ResearchGate*. Available at: www.researchgate.net/publication/349640639_Dissertations_in_20_Steps_-_a_Platonic_Discussion.

2 Writing your front matter

Introduction

Front matter is the name I use for **the essential information that defines your research topic**. This is your **title**, your **aim**, your **objectives** and your **research questions**. Each of these has its own style of writing (known as its **genre**). They also need to be **consistent** with each other in meaning. The relationship between them is shown in Figure 2.1.

We shall explore each of these in turn.

Writing your title

Your title should describe your topic clearly and concisely. It should not be more than about 20 words long. It should also indicate the context for your research in some way so that the reader can see that it can be achieved in the timescale available.

Example

Table 2.1 provides an evaluation of the titles of the four example proposals (see the Acknowledgement in the Preface for more information).

Writing your aim

Your aim should explain what you are seeking to achieve in your research study. A good word to start your aim is "to" as this forces it to be expressed using a verb. It should be consistent with your title but it can explain the context of your work in a little more depth. A suggested maximum length for an aim statement is two sentences or up to 40 words.

DOI: 10.4324/9781003285137-4

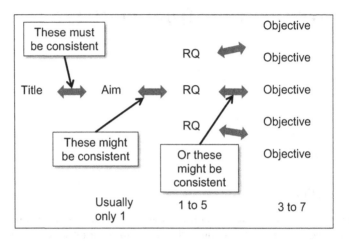

Figure 2.1 Relationship between title, aim, research questions and objectives

Example

Here is Mollie's aim:

> *My main aim for this research project is to research into what loopholes people are finding in taxation policies and any ways to prevent them from happening. I aim to get as many responses as possible from university students, working adults and even pensioners to see what their opinions are and how they feel about the current situations regarding their understanding of taxation policies, loopholes in the policies and the detrimental effect that coronavirus has had on the UK's taxation situation. I hope to be able to explain some methods that the government can use to recover some of their lost taxes from the effects of the pandemic in 2020.*

Here are some observations on Mollie's aim:

- It is consistent with her title and gives more detail (this is a good thing).
- It uses inappropriate personal language – see Chapter 4.
- It is too long for an aim statement (110 words).
- Her proposed research seems to be rather wide-ranging, involving knowledge of loopholes, attitudes towards tax policies and tax avoidance and suggestions of how the UK Government should address these in the context of the Covid-19 pandemic. One, or possibly at most two of these would have been sufficient for a dissertation.

Table 2.1 Example proposal titles and their evaluation

Proposal	Title	Evaluation
Kate	An analysis on the effectiveness of regional integration on economic growth in the East African Community (EAC)	It looks like Kate will be using secondary economic data. It sounds rather broad in scope so it might not be original. Do not introduce or use abbreviations in titles.
Mollie	What should the government do to handle loopholes in their taxation policies and how has COVID-19 affected the way the government should implement their taxation policies in the future?	This title is written as a combination of two related questions. Avoid using rhetoric (asking questions) in titles. Again, the scope of this research sounds rather broad based on just the title.
Tappasiya	Customer satisfaction towards online shopping with reference to Amazon	Again, this research sounds rather broad in scope and unoriginal. What aspects of customer satisfaction are being considered (e.g. price, quality, payment, delivery, customer service, online experience)? What kind of product? Are specific customer markets being identified?
Thomas	Investigating the cross-cultural management issues within a Japanese business' European headquarters: A comparative study between European and Japanese employees in the workplace	This project sounds interesting and suitably narrow in scope. However, it is only achievable if Thomas has access to a suitable source of data (such as a single case study organisation). It might also be helpful to identify a type of cross-cultural management issue, such as communication, or different cultural values or behaviour.

- Mollie's project also involves a broad cross-section of adults. However, it is good that she is thinking about data. Getting as much data as possible is a good strategy in quantitative research but not necessarily in qualitative research. Once Mollie has established her access to data, it might be better for her to narrow her project down to one of these groups.
- Choosing a topic of current concern makes it more interesting to non-specialist readers.
- There are so many parts to Mollie's aim that it really also includes her objectives.

Writing your objectives

Your objectives should be more specific than your aim. They should explain **how** your aim is going to be achieved. This means that carrying out all of your objectives should mean that you have achieved your aim. Like your aim, your objectives should be written as actions, and it is best to start them with the word "to".

Objectives should all be specific to your context. They should also be written in a logical order. There are two main ways this can be achieved:

1   By splitting up the content of your aim into different aspects
2   By considering the different stages of the process of carrying out your research

Example

Here are Thomas' objectives:

- *To conduct a secondary literature review of the Japanese and European professional working cultures*
- *To explore the cultural similarities between Japanese and European workers in the workplace using questionnaires and interviews of these workers in the workplace*
- *To examine how corporate Japanese management communicate with European subordinates in the workplace*
- *To investigate the effectiveness of communication between European and Japanese co-workers in comparison to communication within their own culture*

Here are some observations on Thomas' objectives:

- They are written in the correct genre with four objectives in a logical order starting with the word "to"
- Thomas starts by using the second way of writing objectives then switches to the first way half-way through:
  - His first and second objectives link to stages in the research process as they mention doing a literature review and doing questionnaires and interviews
  - His third and fourth do not and seem to be more to do with the content of his title and aim

Writing your research questions

Research questions are the questions that the study is seeking to answer. Some studies have several research questions whilst others have a main research question which is split into sub-questions. For a proposal, a main research question that is consistent with the title and the aim is sufficient. Alternatively, the research questions might be consistent with the objectives written in the form of questions.

Examples

Kate's main research question is:

> *With regards to the East African Community (EAC), what impact has regional integration had on economic growth in the region?*

This is consistent with her title (see above).
   Mollie has two research questions:

1   *How can the government stop people from taking advantage of loopholes in taxation policies?*
2   *How much of an impact has coronavirus has on the spending of government taxes?*

These questions appear to only cover part of her research topic as defined by her aim. There is no mention of what knowledge taxpayers have or what measures the UK Government should be taking.

Exercises

1   Turn Mollie's title from a combination of two questions into a single description of her topic in about 20 words
2   Rewrite Mollie's aim so it becomes consistent with her title but includes a little more context and is about 40 words long
3   Rewrite Thomas' objectives so that they follow the first main way of writing objectives and do not mention the research process
4   Add some research questions to Mollie's front matter so that they cover all the elements of her existing aim

Part Two

Academic writing

3 Structuring your proposal

Introduction

A proposal is a structured document. As the emphasis of this book is on providing a clear and concise argument for your reader, we recommend that you refer to it as containing **sections** rather than **chapters**.

We recommend only using a **two-level structure** of sections and subsections. A three-level structure of sections, subsections and subsubsections is too much structure for a concise proposal. Furthermore, not every section needs to be divided into subsections.

Essential and optional elements of a proposal

The essential elements of a proposal are:

* A **title**
* An **introduction** section including a background, a problem statement, an aim, objectives and one or more research questions
* A **literature review** section
* A **method and methodology** section (either word on its own is acceptable)
* A **project plan** (this is sometimes included in the methodology section)
* A **reference** list

These are the elements covered in Chapter 2 and Part 3 of this book.
Some optional elements of a proposal are:

* An abstract
* A table of contents (this should come straight after the title page; it is useful with longer proposals)
* A justification or rationale for the study (part of the introduction)
* A discussion on the limitations of the study (part of the introduction)

DOI: 10.4324/9781003285137-6

- A **conceptual framework** (and the end of the literature review or the start of the methodology section)
- A dissemination or impact statement (at the end of the introduction or towards the end of the proposal)
- A budget (an appendix)
- An ethics request form (an appendix)

These may vary according to the requirements of your institution. As this book focuses on the essential elements of proposal writing, the only one of these that it covers is conceptual frameworks in Chapter 10.

Using section numbering

We recommend using a numbering system with sections and subsections as follows:

1 Introduction

  1.1 Background
  1.2 Problem statement
  1.3 Aim and objectives
  1.4 Research questions

2 Literature review

  2.1 Introduction
  2.2 Theme 1
  2.3 Theme 2
  2.4 Discussion

3 Method and Methodology

  3.1 Introduction
  3.2 Conceptual framework
  3.3 Methodology
  3.4 Data collection
  3.5 Data analysis
  3.6 Ethics or limitations

4 Project plan

  References

For more details on the recommended structure of the literature review and the method and methodology sections please refer to Chapters 10 and 12.

It is recommended that you use a different font size and a bold font for section and subsection titles. We also recommend that you do not put any text between a section title and its first subsection title.

Example

Kate's proposal follows the recommended structure quite closely. There are just a few small differences:

- She refers to her sections with a ".0" after them, for example, *1.0 Introduction*, rather than just *1. Introduction*. However, she has used a larger, centred bold font to make them look distinct from her subsection titles.
- She has divided her introduction into five parts instead of four by separating her aim from her objectives (there is nothing wrong with doing this).
- Her literature review follows the recommended structure apart from the final subsection, which she has called a conclusion (again, this is somewhat a matter of taste, but there are more details in Chapter 9).
- Her methodology starts with a paragraph without a subsection title as shown in Figure 3.1. It would have been better if she had labelled this first paragraph as *3.1 Introduction* followed by *3.2 Methodology*.
- She then has subsections on data collection and data analysis but not on ethics or limitations.

3.0 Methodology

The following section covers the methodological approach applied to this research project. The decisions made are informed by the research onion (Saunders et al, 2019) which displays the path taken by a researcher when adopting an effective methodology.

3.1 Methodological approach

A pragmatic philosophy alongside an abductive approach will inform this research project's methodology. As addressing the research problem is of paramount importance, research will be focused on themes that can produce practical outcomes hence the application of a pragmatic philosophy. When determining the effectiveness of the EAC in achieving its objectives, methods that produce tangible results will remain the focal point of analysis.

Figure 3.1 The beginning of Kate's methodology section

- This is followed by her project plan section which contains an unnecessary single subsection *4.1 GANTT chart*. There is no need for subsections if you only have one.
- She has also numbered her references unnecessarily as *5.0 References*.

4 Academic writing style

Introduction: busting a common myth

Some students think academic writing is about using long, complex words and sentences in order to impress academics. This is not true: academic writing is about **clarity** and **simplicity**. Words, sentences and paragraphs should be as easy to understand as possible. They should not use unnecessary words or phrases.

The most important issue in academic writing is to **convey your argument as clearly as possible**. We shall be looking in more depth at paragraph writing in Chapter 6 and argumentation in Chapter 7. We recommend watching Foster's (2019) excellent introductory video to academic writing.

Use the third person, passive voice

It is normally good practice to **avoid personal language** in academic writing. This means not using I, my, you, our, etc. This is often achieved by using the **passive voice** to make claims. The passive voice means a person or object is **having something done to them** rather than them being the agent of a particular action.

Examples

Kate begins the conclusion of her literature review by writing:

> *It can be concluded that, with application of a good export strategy, trade liberalization can have the desired effect on growth.*

By using the phrase "It can be concluded that", Kate is hiding herself as the originator of this conclusion.

DOI: 10.4324/9781003285137-7

Here is another sentence from Kate's literature review:

Nevertheless, the adoption of an effective regional export strategy is greatly stressed.

Kate is again hiding the identity of the people making this claim. In this context it may be assumed to be the wider academic community, not just herself. In the second subsection of her literature review, Tappasiya writes:

It has been stated that a price discount provided to a customer gives them monetary gain as well as increased incentive to purchase the product.

By using the phrase "*It has been stated that*", Tappasiya is hiding the identity of the person who made this claim. However, as this claim is more specific, it would have been better for her to have written this statement more directly by citing the most important authors – please see Chapter 5.

Mollie begins her background by stating:

Throughout this research project I will be looking into three main themes.

Whilst it is good that Mollie is using a thematic approach to writing her background paragraphs (see Chapter 8 for more details), there is no need for her to refer to herself or even to state what she is doing. It would have been better if she had just started introducing her first background theme without any preamble.

At the end of his research rationale and literature gap, Thomas writes:

This has prompted the author to investigate that particular literature gap in this study.

Rather than referring to himself indirectly, it would have been better if Thomas had written a concluding sentence highlighting what the gap in his literature is.

Some dos and don'ts

1. Avoid contractions

Contractions are the first way in which apostrophes are used in English. These should be avoided in academic writing. Words need to be written in full. Contractions such as *don't, doesn't, hasn't, can't* and *it's* should be replaced with *do not, does not, has not, cannot* and *it is*.

2. Use possessive apostrophes correctly

The second use of apostrophes in English is to indicate that something or someone belongs to something or someone. This is known as a **possessive apostrophe**. These should be used in academic writing. There are three forms of possessive apostrophe:

- **A single noun not ending in s** : *'s* needs to be added at the end. For example, *the organisation's role.*
- **A single noun ending in s** : either an apostrophe needs to be added at the end or *'s*. For example, either *the business' aim* or *the business's aim* is acceptable.
- **A plural noun**: an apostrophe should be added at the end. For example, *the industrialised nations' protectionist policies.* This means the protectionist policies of several industrialised nations. The protectionist policies of one nation would be *the industrialised nation's protectionist policies.*

Apostrophes should not be used in any other way in academic writing. A common mistake is to add them to the plural of an acronym. For example, the plural of *SME* is *SMEs* not *SME's.*

3. Introduce acronyms before you use them

An **acronym** is an abbreviation for a proper noun phrase. These should be introduced in full followed by the acronym in brackets. After this the acronym should be used on its own.

For example, Thomas begins his literature review by writing:

> *The Literature Review will firstly introduce the theme of Cross-Cultural Management (CCM) . . .*

Later he writes: *The CCM field related to organisational level studies . . .*

Common acronyms, such as UK, can be assumed. However, do not assume too many technical acronyms as your proposal needs to be accessible to non-specialist readers.

4. Avoid Latin abbreviations

Latin abbreviations should be avoided in academic writing: *e.g.* should be replaced with *for example* or *for instance*; *i.e.* should be replaced with *in other words* or *that is to say*; *etc.* should be replaced with *and so on.*

One Latin abbreviation that you might use is *et al.*, which means *and others*. It is used with several alphabetical referencing systems, such as APA and Harvard. In APA it is used to indicate several authors when a publication has more than three authors. In Harvard style it is used when a publication has more than two authors. It should only be used in the citation and not in the reference list.

For example, Kate is using a variant of the Harvard system. At the beginning of her methodology she writes:

> *The decisions made are informed by the research onion (Saunders et al, 2019).*

This is almost correct. It should be (Saunders et al., 2019) – that is, there should be a full stop after *al*.

However, if Kate was using APA style, she should have written (Saunders, Lewis, & Thornhill, 2019) because et al. is not used unless there are more than three authors.

In the reference list, Kate has written:

> *Saunders, M., Lewis, P., & Thornhill, A. (2019). Research Methods for Business Students. 8th ed. London: Pearson.*

This has a few minor errors but is generally consistent with this variant of Harvard.

For more information on referencing, please refer to Chapter 13.

5. Be consistent when writing numbers

Small whole numbers (ten or less) should be written in words whilst larger numbers, numbers with decimals and percentages should be written in figures.

For example, in her background, Kate has written "*With only two decades of history*". This is correct. It should not be "*With only 2 decades of history*".

Also, in her problem, Kate has written:

> *leading with a projected GDP growth of over 6% in 2020 . . .*

This is also correct. However, *over six percent* would also have been acceptable as six is a small number.

In her methodology, Mollie has written:

> *The questionnaire will be offered to people over the age of 18.*

This is also correct. It would be incorrect to write *18* as *eighteen* as it is larger than ten.

6. Avoid emotive or journalistic language

In academic writing you should avoid language which inspires an emotional reaction from your reader. Do not use colourful metaphors. Avoid using exclamation marks.

Whilst you are trying to interest your reader and you should have some passion about what you are writing, you need to keep your language neutral and unemotive. You are not trying to sell copies of your work as in a newspaper, so the attraction of your writing needs to focus on the interest, clarity and persuasiveness of your ideas, not on your colourful, emotive style of writing about them. Instead, you are trying to provide an academic argument that is **neutral, clear and concise**.

For example, in the second subsection of his literature review, Thomas writes:

> *The urgency to focus on intercommunication efficiency within the work environment has only dramatically increased due to the effects of the COVID-19 pandemic on forcing many employees to work from home and consequently reducing the productivity of team working (van der Lippe, 2019).*

Thomas' use of the word *dramatically* is inappropriate in an academic context as it is emotive. A better word would be *significantly* which does not create such an emotional reaction from the reader. This sentence is also rather long and might be better split into two. If the citation relates to both sentences, then it should be presented in the first sentence, not the second one. This is discussed in the next chapter.

In Tappasiya's literature she writes:

> *Moreover, Amazon's return policy is phenomenal . . .*

The word *phenomenal* is inappropriate in academic writing as it evokes an emotional response. It would have been better if she had said:

> *Moreover, Amazon leads the e-commerce market with its returns policy . . .*

Avoiding subjective writing

Subjective writing often incorporates poor style in some of the ways already described. However, the main issue in subjective writing is with the **poor**

quality of the argument. Specific claims made without evidence to support them are known as beliefs or **opinions**. You should also avoid making value judgments of your own work.

Example

In her methodology, Mollie writes:

> *I feel that using both types of sources will allow me to answer the research topic to the best of my ability.*

Arguments based on feelings are subjective and not persuasive in academic writing, so they should be avoided. It would have been better if she had said something like:

> *Using both types of sources will increase the potential of achieving the research aim within the practical limitations of the project.*

Use hedging

Hedging is the process of using an **appropriate level of caution** when evaluating evidence already presented. This is especially important in a literature review. Phrases such as "it may be argued that" distance the writer from the claim being made. Softening the scope of a claim by using the words such as "some", "often" or "most" is also useful.

Example

Kate writes in her literature review:

> *Despite debates on the existence of a causal link, many economists appreciate that trade liberalization may encourage economic growth through increases in investment, technological spill-overs and access to a larger stock of knowledge (Dodzin and Vamvakidis, 1998).*

Kate is making a cautious claim based on evidence and her evaluation of a scholarly debate. Instead of claiming a causal link she makes a softer claim that *trade liberalization may encourage economic growth* which she asserts is supported by *many economists*, rather than all economists, and for which she provides a citation.

Reference

Foster, Z. (2019) *Constance Hale interview on how to write better* [video]. Available at: www.youtube.com/watch?v=EUNwRpG_5qI.

5 Using evidence

Introduction

All academic writing involves making evidence-based arguments. This is true of proposals. In this chapter we shall look at the need to back up specific claims with evidence, the need to avoid plagiarism, and how to quote and summarise other people's arguments.

Backing up specific claims

Every specific claim you make should be backed up with evidence. In a proposal, evidence takes the form of cited publications.

Examples

In her literature review, Tappasiya writes:

> *According to online service conducted by analysts, it has been observed that more than 64% of e-commerce consumers wait to buy a product until it has gone up for a discount sale, while more than 59 % of these consumers are looking for promo-codes to buy products online (Khan, 2019).*

This sentence contains specific factual information and therefore requires a citation. Tappasiya has correctly added a citation and has used the **indirect citation style** of (author name, year) at the end of a sentence. However, as she is using an alphabetical referencing style, it might have been better if she had used the **direct style** by incorporating Khan's name directly at the start of her sentence like this:

> *According to Khan (2019), more than 64% . . .*

DOI: 10.4324/9781003285137-8

It is also not completely clear what she means by an online service conducted by analysts so perhaps this phrase needs clarifying or removing altogether.

For more information on citing, please refer to Chapter 13.

Avoiding plagiarism

Plagiarism is taking other people's ideas, or parts of their published work, and treating them as your own, or not properly attributing them. Plagiarism is considered unethical, especially in many Western cultures, and may lead to an academic misconduct investigation.

The most common form of plagiarism is **cut and paste**. It is particularly tempting to cut and paste other people's work, especially when you are drafting your own work, but this should be avoided, unless you are planning to use a **direct quote** (see below). The way to overcome this is to **learn how to summarise**.

Possible plagiarism can be examined by using matching software, such as Turnitin (www.turnitin.com/). Such software will generate a report and an overall matching score. Many universities will use matching software such as Turnitin to check their students' work for potential plagiarism. They may also allow their students to submit their draft work to it so they can check their own work before submitting it. However, there is a skill to interpreting the report generated by this software. **There is no safe overall percentage match score** as it depends on the context of the matches. For more information see (Turnitin.com, n.d.).

Quoting

Quoting is **using someone else's work word-for-word and providing a citation**. This is the only form of cut and paste which is permitted in academic writing. The way you quote will depend on the referencing style used by your institution.

Examples

In her literature review Kate writes:

> *Wai Kit Si Tou (2020) attributes this to primary commodities holding a large share of EAC's exports which places the community "in the lower rungs of global value chains" (p. 3), hence stifling regional growth.*

This is a clever combination of a short summary and a direct quote. Kate has correctly put the word-for-word part of the citation in quotation marks and provided a year and a page number. Splitting the year from the page number is acceptable in the Harvard referencing style that she is using. Her only error was to include the author's first name (Wai), which should have been omitted.

In her literature review Mollie writes:

> *Gaspar, V et al has also discussed how coronavirus will affect the future of taxation, "Taxation is profoundly affected by the pandemic. Covid-19 will change taxation – in at least three important ways, with lasting implications."*

Mollie has also correctly included a short direct quote (word-for-word copy) using quotation marks and has provided an in-text citation and a reference in her reference list. She is quoting a news article from the International Monetary Fund, which is a lower level of academic quality than a peer reviewed journal article. However, this was probably acceptable at the time of writing as Covid-19 was a new phenomenon then, and there was little peer reviewed literature written about it.

Her quote is not very long, which is also good, but the introduction to three important ways leaves the reader wondering what they are. Mollie has also added an initial and not included a year in the citation. As it is an online source, there was no need to provide a page number. The correct way to cite this in the Harvard system is:

> *Gaspar et al. (2020) have also discussed . . .*

Also in her literature review, Mollie writes:

> *Collier, R et al, page 794, stated that "In the first phase, while the lockdown is in place and countries are experiencing an acute overall disruption, tax measures can help mitigate the impact of the crisis by providing businesses and households with cash flow in order to avoid a complete collapse of the economy. In the second phase, once the lock-down is lifted, businesses and households are likely to require similar economic support measures."*

Mollie has again correctly used quotation marks and provided a citation. This is a slightly longer quote, which is also acceptable in the short quote style. Again, she has added an initial and left out the year, but she has provided the page number. The correct cite this using the Harvard referencing system is:

> *Collier et al. (2020: 794) stated that, "In . . ."*

You should not over-quote in your writing. It should be a tool in your toolbox. A rule of thumb is **not more than 10% of your citations should be direct quotes**. Quotes are good in your introduction and in the first paragraph of your themes in your literature review as they enable you to borrow someone else's voice to give strength to your own voice.

Summarising

Summarising is the process of rewriting parts of someone else's work **in your own words**. It is the most important skill to master when using evidence. Many students struggle with summarising as they feel their own summaries will not be as good quality as the original writing they are using, and they are tempted to draft their own work by cutting and pasting other people's work. This is a dangerous thing to do, as explained above, as it may lead to plagiarism, even if you correctly cite the authors whose work you are using.

The way to summarise and avoid plagiarism is to **start by writing notes**. You might wish to print out electronic articles and annotate them, or just write notes on a separate sheet of paper. You should then **put the original source to one side** (so you cannot see it) and write up your notes onto your electronic device. By doing this you are breaking the link between the language used in the original source and your summary.

You should then check whether the content of your draft summary has the same meaning as the part of the original source you are summarising. Finally, you should ensure that your summary is of an appropriate length for the relative importance of this source and flows with the rest of your writing.

Example

In her literature review, Kate gives an extended summary of Adam Smith's theory of absolute advantage:

> *Adam Smith, on the other hand, found the concept to lack understanding of the measure of a nation's wealth which he defines as "the annual produce of the land and the labour of the society" (Smith, 1776: 12). He explains that the division of labour creates a specialised workforce which, in turn, produces greater output and increases national wealth. With the introduction of foreign trade, the nation becomes exposed to the larger international market which requires the produce of labour to exceed domestic consumption. This has the effect of enhancing the division of labour and consequently increasing the wealth of a country (Smith, 1776). This then informs Adam Smith's theory of absolute*

> *advantage which states that a nation has absolute advantage over another when it can produce one good with less expenditure on labour.*

Kate's summary includes a direct quote and forms the majority of one of her paragraphs. Her summary is understandable, but without checking a matching report, it is unclear whether she has successfully managed to write the part of her summary outside the quotation marks in her own words.

By using the pronoun "he" in her second sentence, Kate has cleverly connected two sentences together without the need for another citation. It is good practice to only cite a source once in a summary, so there might have been a way she could have removed the second citation. Famous authors, such as Adam Smith, are sometimes referred to by their first name and surname, so this is not an error.

As this is part of Kate's literature review, she might have gone further than this and considered discussing deeper issues, such as: what are the strengths and weaknesses of Smith's theory? Is his theory still relevant or has it been superseded by a more recent one? This might have led Kate into a **critique** of Smith's theory, or into other forms of critical analysis. These are discussed in Chapter 9.

Reference

Turnitin.com (n.d.) *Interpreting the similarity report*. Available at: https://help.turnitin.com/feedback-studio/turnitin-website/instructor/the-similarity-report/interpreting-the-similarity-report.htm.

6 Paragraph writing

Introduction

Paragraph writing is the most important academic writing ability to acquire. That is why it was coloured in red on the academic writing tree picture in Figure 1 in the Introduction.

> *If you can learn how to write good paragraphs, you are more than halfway to becoming a competent academic writer.*

In this chapter we shall provide a definition of paragraphs, consider the ideal length of a paragraph and explore a model structure for paragraph writing. Then we shall look at the use of transitional words and appraise some paragraphs from the example proposals.

Definition

Paragraphs are self-contained pieces of writing made up of sentences. They are a bit like a **mini essay**, often having an introduction, a main body and a conclusion. Paragraphs should be **coherent** and introduce then develop one single **topic**. They should also make one clear **point**.

In order to allow your reader to distinguish between your paragraphs, you should always separate them with some blank space.

Length

In academic writing, paragraphs should cover topics in sufficient depth but not be too long so that the reader can still take them in as a single thought. The ideal length for a paragraph is **about 125 words**. Paragraphs are considered

DOI: 10.4324/9781003285137-9

too short if they are less than about 60 words and too long if they are over 180 about words.

Short paragraphs can indicate you are not writing about your topics in sufficient depth. Long paragraphs might indicate they contain multiple topics or are incoherent.

Structure

Whilst paragraphs need to flow from their beginning to their ending, there is no fixed structure. Rather, there are some general principles and guidance for paragraph writing. Like essays, these principles are based on the simple structure of an introduction, followed by a main body, followed by a conclusion.

Introduction

It is good practice to start each paragraph with a **topic sentence**, which makes a general point and introduces the subject that rest of the paragraph will be about.

A **common error** students make in academic writing is to **put a specific assertion in their first sentence** which is backed up with a citation. There are two problems with doing this:

1   It is unclear what the scope of the argument in the rest of the paragraph is going to be.
2   It is difficult to separate your voice from that of the author(s) you have cited. This is particularly an issue in literature reviews and will be discussed later.

This is why it is a good idea to start paragraphs with general claims not requiring a citation.

Main body

After introducing the topic of your paragraphs, you might wish to explain this further and provide some evidence about this topic or one or more examples. There should be some logical flow to the order you present your sentences. You should ensure that the argument is not too long or complicated, and the amount of evidence you cite is sufficient to support your specific claims, but not too much for your reader to take in. This requires critical thinking to have to confidence to emphasise the more important evidence.

Conclusion

You should round up your paragraphs at the end with some sort of conclusion. Sometime, this is the best place to write the main point of your paragraphs. You might link to the subject of the section that your paragraph forms a part of. You might reiterate the point you made at the start of the paragraph based on the argument you have presented, or you might create an awareness of an issue you will explore in the next paragraph.

Using transitional words

The argument you present in your paragraphs can be organised or structured using transitional words which often appear at the start of sentences. These act as a 'glue' to stick your sentences together, although they are not required in between every pair of sentences. Transitional words can help your reader to understand the logic behind your argument and make it flow better.

> *The clearer you present your argument, the clearer your own thinking will be about the subject.*

Transitional words come in different types. Table 6.1 provides some common transitional words split into types.

Examples

Here is a paragraph from Kate's literature review:

> *In the case of the EAC, the elimination of trade barriers has had clear positive effects on regional trade. Since the beginning of the union,*

Table 6.1 Examples of different types of transitional word

To signal	Examples
Contrast	But, whereas, yet, still, however, although, despite, on the contrary, conversely
Addition	Furthermore, subsequently, besides, next, moreover, also, similarly
Example	For example, for instance, an illustration of, specifically
Time or place	Afterwards, earlier, at the same time, currently, subsequently, later, simultaneously, so far, until now, while
Conclusion	Therefore, in short, in essence, thus, in other words, in conclusion, consequently, as a result, accordingly, nevertheless
Sequence	Then, next, first, second, third, etc.

intra-EAC trade has accounted for an increasing percentage of GDP among member states. Rwanda, for example, managed to double its total trade value to Kenya from US$207 million to US$550 million only a year after joining the union (Umulisa, 2020). Despite this, low EAC exports to the world remain a key constraint to growth. Wai Kit Si Tou (2020) attributes this to primary commodities holding a large share of EAC's exports which places the community "in the lower rungs of global value chains" (p. 3), hence stifling regional growth. To counter this, he recommends boosting export performance through development of manufactured products related to the existing production factors. Nevertheless, the adoption of an effective regional export strategy is greatly stressed.

This paragraph is 145 words long, which is within the acceptable range. It contains a generally understandable and coherent argument. She begins with a general topic sentence without a citation. This indicates that her paragraph is going to be about trade within the East African Community (EAC). However, it is actually about trade both within and outside of the EAC, so this might have been improved.

Her second sentence sounds more specific and might have benefitted from a citation, although it is still fairly general. However, her third sentence gives a more specific example of Rwanda and does contain a citation. She then uses the transition word "despite" to introduce the opposite side of her argument, which relates to trade outside of the EAC. This is explained in the following two sentences based on a citation. She starts her final sentence with the word "nevertheless" to indicate that she is drawing her argument to a conclusion. The main point of her paragraph is about the need for a regional export strategy.

Here is a paragraph from Thomas' literature review:

Cross Cultural Management is generally defined by Adler (2002) as the describing and comparing of organisational behaviour within and across both countries and cultures whilst also attempting to comprehend and enhance interactions between a business' multicultural stakeholders. The CCM field related to organisational level studies have been researched vastly over the years (Romani, 2018) in response to a more globalised world (Chanda, 2004). Although, Primecz (2016) suggested that while cross cultural management has been researched and defined widely, little research has been conducted within the power relations of different cultures and the impact it has within the working environment. An objective of this study aims to study the power context of Japanese management on European subordinates particularly in terms of intercommunication.

This paragraph is 121 words long, which is about the recommended length. However, it only contains four sentences, indicating that the sentences themselves are rather long and complex. However, the content of this paragraph is generally understandable and coherent.

Thomas' argument flows from defining Cross Cultural Management (CCM) in the first sentence to justifying an objective of his study relating, to a particular kind of CCM in the last sentence. However, it is recommended that the reappraisal of objectives is best left until the discussion at the end of a literature review.

If his last sentence was therefore to be moved to the discussion, the main point of his paragraph could be the claim he makes in the third sentence about the lack of research on power relations between different cultures and their impact on the working environment. Whilst this claim is well justified by a relevant citation, it might have benefitted from further discussion which could have explored this issue in a little more depth. His main point could then have been a more balanced and cautious conclusion about this perceived gap in the literature and how it relates to his context.

One of the problems with Thomas' literature review is that it is over-structured as it contains subsections. This is not advised in a short proposal like his. The consequence of this is his subsection on Cross Cultural Management only contains a single paragraph. This has made it difficult for him to explore this issue in sufficient depth. These issues will be discussed further in the next chapter on Argumentation Styles, and in Chapter 9 on Literature Reviews.

7   Argumentation

Introduction

Arguments form the backbone of academic writing. Argument writing complements paragraph writing. It is important to understand that there are two main styles of arguments and when they should be used. If you can learn how to plan your arguments in advance, then it can save you a lot of effort.

Two styles

There are two fundamental styles of argumentation known as **single argument/opinion** and **discursive**.

Single argument/opinion style

The single argument/opinion style is **adversarial**. It can be likened to the **council for the prosecution** or defence in a courtroom whose role is to put forward one side of the argument. The argument presented might still contain evidence which challenges the main claim being made, but this is always argued against. The argument is usually presented as a claim from the beginning when the topic is introduced. Supporting evidence is then presented and the conclusion basically agrees with the claim made at the beginning, although it may clarify it somewhat.

The single argument/opinion style argument should be used in most of your proposal introduction as it should describe the background context and provide a rationale (one-sided argument) for choosing your topic. It should also be used in your methodology as your focus should be on explaining and justifying the choices you have made about methodology and method and explaining their application.

DOI: 10.4324/9781003285137-10

Discursive style

The discursive style argument is very different. In terms of the court meta-phor, it can be likened to the **judge** or the **jury** whose role is to weigh up evidence on both sides of the argument. A subject is introduced neutrally at the start, rather than a claim about it. Evidence is then presented on both sides of the argument, then a cautious conclusion is drawn at the end which **could not be anticipated** from the beginning.

The discursive style argument is very useful in literature reviews. It enables you to distance yourself from the evidence you are presenting and evaluate conflicting evidence in the process of exploring deeper questions. A common error in academic writing is an over-use of the single argument/ opinion style in literature reviews.

Examples

Single argument/opinion argument

Here is an example of an adversarial argument from Mollie's literature review:

> *The government furlough schemes that have been running since the beginning of the pandemic have resulted in massive government spend-ing, and are going to be running up until at least the end of February 2021, (KPMG, 2020). This will result in a negative effect on other funding that the government has got to provide in the UK. The government will need to try and cut down on the amount of people who are avoiding taxes, whether it is through paying into trusts, paying salaries out to people, or even paying extra money into pensions to avoid a higher tax band.*

Mollie is essentially **describing** government furlough schemes and **making claims** about their implications rather than **exploring deeper issues** about this subject, such as:

- What alternatives did the government have?
- How did the UK Government's approach compare with that of other similar countries going through a similar health crisis?
- Are there any positive effects of this potential reduction in government spending in other areas?
- What other measures might the government use to try to avoid a reduction in tax income?

Exploring some of these issues might have led to a discursive style argument being more appropriate.

Discursive argument

Kate uses a discursive style argument in one of the paragraphs in her literature review:

> *Modern theories offer a more dynamic and empirical approach to the subject matter and, most importantly, acknowledge the varying effects of trade openness on divergent economies. Despite debates on the existence of a causal link, many economists appreciate that trade liberalization may encourage economic growth through increases in investment, technological spill-overs and access to a larger stock of knowledge (Dodzin and Vamvakidis, 1998). With regards to developing economies, there is little to no evidence to suggest positive effects of trade openness on economic growth. Spanu (2013) explains that although countries which encourage openness tend to experience growth, developing nations find themselves in a unique situation where openness is rendered ineffective due to the industrialised nations' protectionist policies, which stifle their exports. Singh (2010) adds that positive effects of trade, such as technological spill-overs, mainly occur between developed and developing nations between which there are technological gaps hence emphasizing the extent to which these protectionist policies harm developing nations. Despite this, Spanu (2013) maintains that trade liberalization could promote economic growth in developing nations with macroeconomic stability and good governance.*

Whilst Kate's opening sentence is a bit difficult to take in, she is making a general claim about the topic of the rest of her paragraph, which is the relationship between trade openness and economic growth. After presenting a cautious claim about the existence of this relationship, she applies her argument to her context of developing economies. This leads her to make a balanced conclusion in the final sentence. This conclusion could not have been anticipated in advance, which is consistent with discursive style arguments.

Argument planning

Keen students often waste much time by over-writing and then trying to cut down their draft. Other students write what comes into their heads without a plan. This often means not knowing what you are trying to say and leads to your paragraphs being unclear in flow and direction and not making a single clear point.

The answer to these problems is to **plan your argument in advance**. Here's how to do it:

- For each section of your proposal, calculate an estimated wordcount based on the overall wordcount and their relative importance. For example, our undergraduate students need to write a 2,000-word proposal, so we recommend a literature review of about 800 words.
- For sections longer than 1,000 words, decide how they will be split into subsections and calculate an estimated wordcount for each subsection.
- For sections under 1,000 words, divide the estimated wordcount by 125 to give you an estimated number of paragraphs. For example, for our undergraduate students, this would lead to between six and seven paragraphs for their literature reviews.
- Now imagine you are **giving a presentation** to some of your fellow students about the subject of your section or subsection and you have **one slide** to present some **bullet points**.
- Write one bullet point for each paragraph.
- Now evaluate your points: are they in the right order and are they equally important?
- Once you have clarified the points you are trying to make, you just need to draft one paragraph around each point.

A diagram of this process is shown in Figure 7.1. It includes some additional advice on how to write an introduction and a conclusion for a longer section split into themes.

By following this method, your argument will be clearer, and you will avoid over-writing. This will also save you time. It will also help you to **socialise your writing process** as you will be imagining someone listening to your presentation of your argument.

Example

Here is an example of an argument plan presentation for the introduction section of one of my own research papers (Samuels and Haapasalo, 2012). This section is 1,075 words long and is split into ten paragraphs.

- *There is a major problem with older students' engagement with mathematics*
- *There has been a rapid increase in the adoption of new (mobile) personal technologies by contemporary learners*

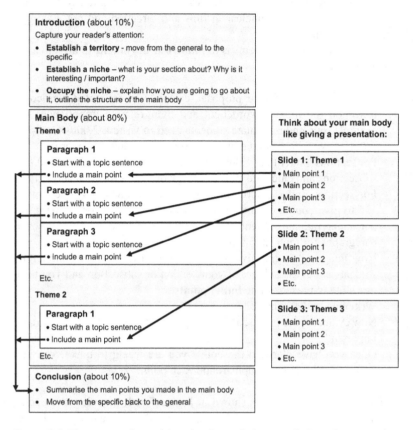

Figure 7.1 The presentation writing planning technique applied to a longer section split into themes

- *But the educational sector has been slow to adapt their approaches in view of this increase*
- *There is also a need to emphasise practices for informal mathematics rather than formal mathematics*
- *There have been past successes with turtle graphics robots and the LOGO programming language for teaching basic mathematics to younger children*
- *Research into whether using physical robots or a virtual programming language is better is inconclusive*
- *There is a potential application of robotics with older students*
- *It is now possible to animate virtual robots within richer mathematical environments*

- *Aim of paper: to combine real and virtual robotics with older students to motivate mathematics engagement and learning*
- *Outline: rationale; pedagogical approach; evaluation criteria; feasibility and technological evaluation; pedagogical evaluation*

This example is slightly on the long side for this technique, but you should be able to follow this argument even if you do not know very much about the subject. It is best to use this technique to plan arguments between three and seven paragraphs long.

Exercise

Based on the suggested proposal outline from Chapter 3:

1   Introduction

  1.1 Background
  1.2 Problem statement
  1.3 Aim and objectives
  1.4 Research questions

2   Literature review

  2.1 Introduction
  2.2 Theme 1
  2.3 Theme 2
  2.4 Discussion

3   Method and Methodology

  3.1 Introduction
  3.2 Conceptual framework
  3.3 Methodology
  3.4 Data collection
  3.5 Data analysis
  3.6 Ethics or limitations

4   Project plan

Use your total wordcount that you are aiming to write for your proposal to estimate the number of paragraphs you need for each section and subsection based on an average paragraph length of 125 words.

Then create a draft presentation with one bullet point per paragraph to provide the argument structure for your whole proposal.

Then use your plan to draft your proposal.

Reference

Samuels, P. C. and Haapasalo, L. (2012) Real and virtual robotics in mathematics education at the school-university transition. *International Journal of Mathematical Education in Science and Technology*, 43(3), pp. 285–301.

Part Three

Writing the rest of your proposal

8 Writing the rest of your introduction

Introduction

Now that we have covered topic selection and the basics of academic writing, we can focus on writing the rest of your proposal. In this chapter we will look at writing the rest of your introduction. We have already covered front matter writing in Chapter 2, so we just need to cover the remaining elements. The most important of these are the **background** and the **problem statement**. Together they form your **rationale**. We begin by discussing these elements and then move on to the other optional elements which you might choose to present later on in this section.

Writing your background

Your background should provide your reader with a basic understanding of the key concepts which are being combined together or applied to create your research topic. You should write one paragraph for each concept which should include a definition and a basic factual description.

A useful metaphor for background writing is the *What 3 Words* app (https://what3words.com/). This app allows you to pinpoint any three-metre-sided square on the earth's surface using a unique combination of three English words. In the same way, it should be possible for you to define a unique research topic by combining **three, or at most four, distinct fundamental concepts**. You should aim to write one paragraph on each concept.

Another metaphor for background writing is a **big cat scent marking its territory**. Each paragraph in your background and its associated topic is like a tree or rock that you need to "scent mark" by demonstrating that you have a good basic understanding of that subject.

DOI: 10.4324/9781003285137-12

Example

Kate's proposal title is, "*An analysis on the effectiveness of regional integration on economic growth in the East African Community*". Her background contains three paragraphs covering the following topics:

- Regional integration in developing nations and associated trade agreements post-World War II
- The East African Community (EAC) regional integration agreement
- The aims of the EAC and how they are being achieved

Her choice of first paragraph topic makes sense as it provides a more general context for her research topic. Her second and third paragraph topics are also relevant, but they are similar, and it might have been better to combine these together.

What is missing is a background paragraph on evaluating the relationship between trade agreements and economic growth. This should only be descriptive at this stage. A deeper discursive style evaluation can be left for the literature review.

Writing your problem statement

Your problem statement should connect your background with your chosen research topic. It should be shorter than your background, so two paragraphs might be sufficient. The argumentation style of your problem statement should be adversarial as you are providing a rationale for why your topic is **interesting**, **relevant**, **original**, and **viable**, as explained in Chapter 1.

One technique for problem statement writing is to combine together the concepts introduced in two of the paragraphs from your background. Another technique is to include the context of your research associated with the data you are proposing to collect.

The conclusion to your argument in your problem statement should be your aim. You should not mention your proposed study until this point.

Example

Thomas' proposal is entitled "*Investigating the Cross-Cultural management issues within a Japanese Business' European headquarters: A comparative study between European and Japanese employees in the workplace*". After his background, his proposal has two paragraphs in Section 1.3 entitled, "Research Rationale & Literature Gap":

- In his first paragraph he introduces cross-cultural management research
- In his second paragraph he explores differences between organisational culture and national culture with reference to his chosen data collection context (multinational Japanese companies with European employees)

Here is Thomas' second paragraph:

However, research has suggested that organisational culture can differ from national culture depending on the size of the business among other factors (Nazarian, 2014). This study will attempt to contribute to the cross-cultural management literature by investigating the cross-cultural issues focusing within a multinational company between Japanese and European employees. When searching the CCM literature in this area, few studies have been fulfilled in relation to comparing Japanese and European co-workers in the same workplace, particularly in Japanese multinational businesses. Of the studies that exist, many are respectively too old such as Lincoln's (1995) Cross cultural case studies of Japanese companies across Germany and Brannen's (2000) research into culture within Japanese-German joint ventures. According to Søderberg (2002), Literature within cross cultural management needs to be rethought in a fast-changing globalising world, suggesting more recent 21st century studies are necessary to rejuvenate the CCM research pool, punctually outdating many of the studies from the year 2000 and older. This has prompted the author to investigate that particular literature gap in this study.

Whilst both paragraphs are well written and relevant, their topics are not ideal choices for a problem statement. This may have been because Thomas was not writing a problem statement, although his assignment brief stated that he should.

His first paragraph topic is a bit too general for a problem statement and might have been better placed in his background. Perhaps a better choice of first paragraph could have been something about his context, such as a description of Japanese businesses with European headquarters (addressing questions such as: when did they start? how many of them are there? how much are they worth? what business sectors are they mostly in? and what are the most influential examples?)

His second paragraph provides a very good summary of his research gap, but his topic is a bit complex – it might have been better to move his first sentence to the background and to focus the rest of paragraph in the problem statement on organisational culture with reference to Thomas' chosen context.

Also notice how Thomas refers to his study near the start of his second paragraph. In a problem statement such references should only come right at the end. His last sentence should also be rephrased as it is not good practice to refer to yourself in the third person as "the author" – you should provide an objective argument using the passive voice to hide the person proposing to undertake the research.

Additional parts

Additional subsections of an introduction you might include are:

- A **rationale** or **justification** for your study – however, there is no real need for this if you write your background and problem statement well. If your institution requires you to write it, then it should just be a short section that reiterates the argument you have already presented in these sections.
- **Thesis** – a statement of what you are trying to show. This is not appropriate in all studies, and you should be careful **not to sell a solution** as you need to focus on the problem you have identified in your proposal introduction, not a solution to it. This might be a single sentence, or it might be up to one paragraph. Furthermore, I would strongly recommend **not including hypotheses** in an introduction as these make assumptions about the type of research you are proposing to undertake and the type of data you are planning to collect, which can only be adequately explored in your methodology section.
- **Limitations** – you might want to reflect on potential limitations to your achievement of your aim. However, these might be better placed in your methodology section.
- **Significance** or **potential impact** – these might be relevant here. You should write these **modestly** using phrases such as "It is hoped that this research will be of some benefit to . . .", or ". . . make a small contribution to . . .".
- **Outline** of the rest of your proposal, although there is no real need for this as your primary readers should already know the structure of proposals.

Example

The only example of an additional part in the example proposal introductions is Mollie's limitations subsection:

> *When working through my research project there will no doubt be things that limit my investigation and I will have to try and overcome*

them as best I can. The first being the participants in my questionnaire. Some people may wish to withdraw from the questionnaire, which they can do at any point – however I will need to ensure that I have enough information to make reasonable conclusions. I will also have people who wish to remain anonymous throughout the process, which will not be a limitation, however it will be harder to categorise the findings. Another limitation may be that people may not be giving accurate information, which could make my findings incorrect. The questionnaires will be made so that they are easy to understand and complete so that people do not lose interest.

Mollie's argument would have been better placed in her methodology as the issues she has identified are mainly to do with her proposed data collection. She has also used first person language extensively ("I", "my"), which should be avoided in academic writing.

9   Literature reviews

Introduction

The purpose of your proposal literature review is **to provide your reader with a focused critical discussion** of the most relevant research relating to your chosen topic. The literature review is perhaps the most complex section of your proposal to produce, so this is the longest chapter in the book. However, as your introduction will be read first and contains the front matter defining your project, it might be considered even more important. Nevertheless, writing a good literature review demonstrates your understanding of the most relevant published research literature in your field, which is one of the important things proposal markers are looking for.

A literature review in a business research proposal should be more than an **annotated bibliography**, which is simply a sequence of single paragraph summaries of research studies. Instead, it should be organised into a few key **themes**, which are broader research areas than your chosen research topic. Your choice of themes could be similar to your paragraph topics in your background. The process of creating a thematic literature review is illustrated in Figure 9.1.

We continue this chapter by considering some general principles of creating a literature review. Next, we explore how you can obtain suitable research evidence. Next, we will discuss how to choose your themes. It is important to include some theory within your review so after this we look at different ways of doing this. The main thing that distinguishes a literature review from a background is the inclusion of **critical analysis,** so what this is and how to do it is explored next. Finally, we consider how best to conclude your literature review.

General principles

It is important to **capture your reader's attention** at the start of your literature review. You could consider including answers to questions such as,

DOI: 10.4324/9781003285137-13

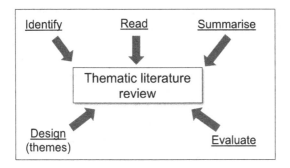

Figure 9.1 The thematic literature review creation process
Source: (Samuels, 2021)

"Why do you find this research project interesting?" and, "Why do you think it is important?" (although your answers should use the third person passive voice).

Your review should start with an **introduction** which states its **purpose** and **scope** and introduces the themes you are going to include. One of the secrets of academic writing is to **answer the question that is in the mind of your reader** without stating what it is.

It is important to **have a plan** of how you are going to write your review. Apart from the steps mentioned below, this should include:

- Moving from a **general** context to the **specific** context of your research
- Using **subsection headings** to structure your review; however, this should not be overdone as it is important to get into a flow in your writing in order to explore deeper issues
- Including relevant **theories**
- Using **visual representations**, such as tables which combine evidence from different sources, or illustrative figures; these will assist your readers who are more visual thinkers than verbal thinkers
- Finish with a discussion that refocuses on your research questions

Obtaining evidence

With the advent of the internet, most literature searching is done online nowadays and does not require entering a physical library. Ways of doing this include:

- Using Google Scholar (https://scholar.google.co.uk/). As already mentioned in Chapter 1, the Google Scholar search engine is very useful in the topic selection process, but it can also be used at the start of the literature search process. Some institutions provide deep links to documents available in their e-library provided that you first log in to them in your internet browser. As already mentioned in the example in Chapter 1, you should use a variety of keywords for the same concept, narrow searches down with quotation marks to create phrases and consider restricting the years of publication, such as in the last 20 years. Once you identify research of interest, the **cited by** link is useful for measuring the relative importance of published research and finding additional articles which cite this article that were published more recently.

- Using your library's **meta search engine**. Most UK universities provide a front end to all their electronic resources, known as a meta search engine. This will link to their databases and electronic journals. The same principles apply as for Google Scholar; you may find that the interface has additional features, but it may be slightly more difficult to use. You may have been trained or there may be training materials available, or you may wish to seek out your subject area librarian to help you use this tool effectively.

- Your library may also subscribe to some research **databases**. These are normally specific to certain subject areas. Business databases may contain other forms of business publications, such as company reports or marketing reports. The same search principles apply as for Google Scholar above.

- Once you start to obtain some relevant sources you might also start to identify some **electronic journals** which are particularly relevant to your topic area by identifying common places where these sources are published. You might then search directly within these journals. A suitable timeframe for such a search is **the last ten years**.

You also need to consider **what** you are looking for and **how to choose** the best literature to include. The first thing to decide is the **overall purpose** of your review. Secondly, you need to decide on the scope you will be looking at.

Example

Kate's proposal is about regional integration and economic growth in the East African Community. Should she limit her literature research to articles published about regional integration in Sub-Saharan Africa or should she look at similar regions in other continents which include developing countries? The answer may depend on how much literature is available about the former.

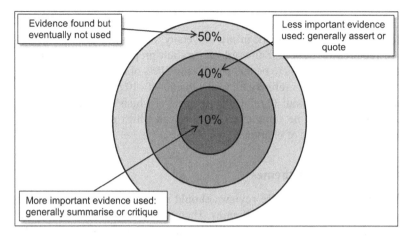

Figure 9.2 The 50–40–10 principle

Once you have identified a sufficient amount of relevant literature, you need to decide how to choose what to look at in more depth and then eventually what to include using some type of citation. I like to use a rule of thumb for this which I call the **50–40–10 principle**, as illustrated in Figure 9.2.

A mistake made by some keen students is to find and read too much evidence in detail. They end up confused, work too hard and do not get the mark they deserve. The 50–40–10 principle indicates that you should aim to only **find about twice as much evidence as you eventually use**.

A second mistake some students make is to treat all citations at the same level of importance, such as in an annotated bibliography. This will also not lead to a good mark as it does not demonstrate critical thinking. You should not aim to write the same amount of text about each reference. The most important evidence should have a longer form of citation, such as a summary or a critique. The less important evidence should have a shorter citation, such as an indirect citation backing up a factual claim, a direct quote or a single sentence summary. The ratio of the most important evidence to the less important evidence should be about 4:1.

Another issue to consider is how many references you should have in your literature review. My advice is as follows:

- Your literature review should be about 35%–40% of your proposal wordcount.
- The density of citations in a literature review as normally higher than in other forms of academic writing. I would recommend about **20 references per 1,000 words**.

Example

In the school where I work in my university, our undergraduate students are required to write 2,000-word dissertation proposals. We recommend their literature reviews to be 800 words long (40% of their total wordcount) and contain about 15 references. Using the 50–40–10 principle, this would mean identifying about 30 relevant references of which 15 were used. Three of these 15 would be summarised or critiqued whilst the other 12 would have a shorter form of citation.

Deciding on your themes

Whilst proposal literature reviews should be quite concise, it is still a good idea to split them into **themes**. Themes are broader areas than your chosen topic. They are often similar in scope to the topics of paragraphs in your background (see Chapter 8). Themes can also be viewed as perspectives which have their own literature base. They should be distinct from each other, or they should not overlap very much. The combination of your themes should provide alternative perspectives for viewing your topic.

You may already have an idea of which themes you want to include, or they may become clear from your literature review. A technique I recommend is to **draw a concept map** of your literature review and **create a post-it note** for each of your references (including the author, year and a brief description), then try to **stick the post-it notes** to the concept map – see Figure 9.3. The clustering of the notes on the map might indicate possible themes.

Your themes should also have an appropriate scope with a sufficient number of references, but not too many.

Example

Kate's literature review is divided into two themes entitled *Trade openness and growth* and *The case of East Africa*. Both themes are about 350 words long. She also has a short introduction at the start and a short conclusion at the end. This is appropriate for an 800-word literature review.

However, the main way Kate could have improved her themes would have been to consider regional integration and economic growth separately in two themes. Then she could have explored the application to East Africa in a longer discussion at the end. She might also have limited her literature review in each theme, such as only looking at economic growth in Sub-Saharan Africa.

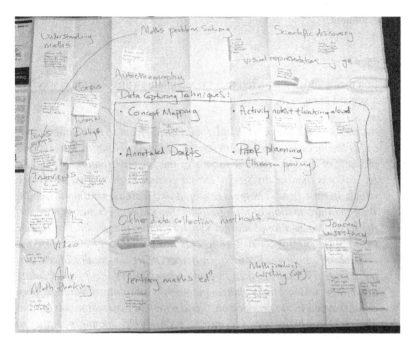

Figure 9.3 Example concept map with post-it notes (from my own research)

Including theory

Literature reviews should also include **theoretical perspectives**. A theory is a collection of concepts which explain how a phenomenon works. They are usually well regarded in the research community and remain relevant for a longer period of time than most primary research studies (which are known as **empirical literature**).

You can include theory in different ways:

- A theory might be relevant to your whole review. You could then begin your review with a **theoretical framework**, which would become your first theme. You should try to move beyond simply introducing and describing a theory by attempting to answer deeper questions about it, such as "how does it apply to my context?", and "what are its strengths and weaknesses?". Please see the next section for more information.
- There may be one or more theories relevant to one of your themes. You might then discuss these in the first paragraph of your theme.

• You might refer to a less important theory in passing within your argument.

Example

The first theme of Kate's literature review contains a theoretical perspective in her second paragraph.

> *Adam Smith, on the other hand, found the concept to lack understand-ing of the measure of a nation's wealth which he defines as "the annual produce of the land and the labour of the society" (Smith, 1776: 12). He explains that the division of labour creates a specialised workforce which, in turn, produces greater output and increases national wealth. With the introduction of foreign trade, the nation becomes exposed to the larger international market which requires the produce of labour to exceed domestic consumption. This has the effect of enhancing the division of labour and consequently increasing the wealth of a coun-try (Smith, 1776). This then informs Adam Smith's theory of absolute advantage which states that a nation has absolute advantage over another when it can produce one good with less expenditure on labour. Therefore, for better use of resources, each country should specialise in the production of the good which it has absolute advantage in (Schum-acher, 2012).*

Kate has adopted an interesting approach in this paragraph by arguing against the first paragraph in her theme, which appears to be mainly sup-ported by empirical literature. Although Smith's theory of absolute advan-tage is very old, it is still viewed as being relevant. It would be interesting for the reader to know more specifically whether Schumacher has updated Smith's theory or applied Smith's theory to her context. Perhaps it might have been better if she had started this theme with Smith's theory, then cri-tiqued it, then considered alternative perspectives.

Kate also includes a second time-proven theory in the third paragraph of this theme by David Ricardo. She would have received credit for intro-ducing and discussing relevant theories as well as empirical literature. But perhaps she could have brought her argument to a clearer conclusion at the end of this theme.

Including critical analysis

Many students ask me what critical analysis is and whether their writ-ing includes it. A common criticism of literature reviews is that they lack critical analysis. There is a debate amongst researchers and educators on this subject. There are different perspectives on what critical analysis is. My view is that critical analysis is different in nature between different subject areas, but it has some common features across all subjects.

Critical analysis is a specific type of **critical thinking**. Ennis (2011) defines critical thinking as, "reasonable and reflective thinking focused on deciding what to believe or do". Critical analysis is **the application of critical thinking to the evaluation of research evidence**. A popular study book on critical thinking is by Cottrell (2017). However, if you are looking for a less skills-orientated approach to critical analysis, I would recommend Moon's (2007) book.

When including critical analysis in a proposal literature review, a very useful device is a **discursive style paragraph**. This is a single paragraph argument which introduces a subject area, presents evidence from different perspectives, then evaluates this evidence in the form of a cautious conclusion, which uses **hedging**. Please refer to Chapters 5, 7 and 8 for more information on hedging, paragraph writing and discursive arguments.

Example

Here is an example of a discursive style paragraph from an unpublished extract from one of my own pieces of writing. I have annotated each sentence to explain its purpose.

> *[Topic sentence] There is disagreement between researchers over the appropriateness of a deep approach to studying within STEM subjects. [First view] There is some alignment between the deep learning construct and relational understanding construct in Skemp's (1962) schematic learning theory, which he promotes as being particularly effective in mathematics education, providing evidence of improved retention of concepts. [Evidence] In a study of 236 first year undergraduate mathematics students in Australia, Crawford et al. (1993) demonstrated a significant ($p < 0.001$) association between a cohesive conception of mathematics (similar to Skemp's relational understanding) and a deep approach to studying, and a fragmented conception of mathematics (similar to Skemp's instrumental understanding) and a surface approach to studying. However, [Alternative view] Kirschner et al. (2006) argue against the effectiveness of discovery-based learning and constructivism, providing evidence that students learn more deeply from strongly guided learning experiences. In addition, [Another view] Beattie et al. (1997) also argue against the universal appropriateness of a deep approach to studying where learning requires the practising*

of skills and processes, as is common in STEM subjects. In summary, [Evaluation] a deep approach to studying does not appear to be universally appropriate in STEM contexts.

There are many features to this paragraph which are instructive:

- It is a little bit long but just about acceptable
- It starts with a topic sentence that introduces the scope of the paragraph
- It then presents evidence from different sides of the argument
- It uses **transitional words and phrases** (however, in addition, in summary) to indicate to the reader how the argument is developing
- It is evidence based and makes a distinction between theory (Skemp) and an empirical study based on a theory (Crawford et al.)
- It has a cautious conclusion at the end which evaluates the presented evidence (using hedging)
- The conclusion leaves the reader thinking, "why doesn't this approach always work?" – this could be explored in more depth in another paragraph, such as in the final dissertation

There are other forms of critical analysis, but I believe the discursive style paragraph is the most useful technique for presenting critical analysis in a proposal in a concise manner.

Another important way of viewing critical analysis is to consider the **depth of questions** behind your writing. As I already mentioned, one of the secrets of academic writing is to answer the questions in your reader's mind without stating them:

- **Shallower questions** often start with *who, what, where* and *when*
- **Deeper questions** often start with **how** and **why**
- It is recommended that you should start with shallow questions then move towards deeper questions

Example

Tappasiya's literature review contains a brief theme entitled *Consumer behaviour in regards to offers and discounts*. If her theme was to be expanded into several paragraphs, it might cover answer to questions such as:

- What are special offers and discounts?
- When were they invented and by whom?
- What are the most common types of special offer and discount relevant to Tappasiya's context (Amazon)?

- Why does Amazon use these approaches?
- What are the most relevant theories which explain consumer behaviour regarding discounts and special offers? What are their relative strengths and weaknesses?
- How could these theories be applied to the context of Amazon to evaluate their approaches and suggest improvements?

Concluding your review

You should conclude your review with a critical discussion which focuses on your chosen topic. You can begin this by **summarising the findings from each of your themes** and then applying them to your specific context. There should be a smaller number of references which are directly relevant to your own research which you should cite here.

The summary of the relationship between the main concepts in your critical discussion could be represented in the form of a figure, known as a **conceptual framework**. This is explored in the next chapter.

Finally, you can **reappraise your research questions** from your introduction. This will connect your introduction to the findings of your literature review and create a rationale for carrying out your research project which will lead into your next section.

In other words, you should be arguing:

- This is what I said I wanted to answer (as stated in my introduction)
- This is what is already known about the subject (the findings of your literature review, which are often inconclusive, or from a different related context)
- Therefore, this is why I need to carry out this research

Obviously, you should not use first person language like this, but this is essentially what you should be trying to argue in order to persuade your reader of the importance of your study.

Example

Thomas' proposal has the most extensive conclusion to his literature review. It contains three short paragraphs:

- His first paragraph makes an interesting claim of a research gap amongst Western scholars which appears to summarise the findings of his second theme.

- In his second paragraph, he returns to the subject of power relations which he introduced in his first theme and combines this with his current context of doing research during the Covid-19 pandemic.
- His final paragraph contains a discussion of an appropriate theoretical framework for exploring disputes in cross-cultural management. Whilst this is interesting, this argument might have been better placed earlier in his review.

Thomas could have written a clearer conclusion to his review by following the principles explained above, which would have made it easier for the reader/marker to have understood his initial findings and how this justifies the need for his research.

Exercise

Use the evaluation sheet in Table 9.1 to assess your draft literature review.

Table 9.1 Literature review evaluation sheet

Aspect	Evaluation
Overall length about 35–40% of total wordcount	
Starts with an introduction	
Purpose and scope explained in introduction	
Rest of structure: two themes followed by a discussion	
Appropriate choice of themes	
Choice of themes introduced/justified in the introduction	
Each theme introduced/explained at the start its subsection	
Paragraphs have clear topics	
Paragraphs make clear points	
Paragraphs are the right length (60–180 words)	
Use of transitional words within paragraphs to indicate argument development	
Use of hedging (cautious conclusions based on evidence presented)	
Each claim backed up with evidence	
Length of citations distinguishes between more and less important evidence	
Use of a variety of citation styles (indirect, quotes, short summaries and longer summaries)	
Inclusion of theory (e.g. theoretical framework, theme-specific theories, or localized theories)	
Inclusion of critical analysis (discursive argument addressing deeper questions)	
Conclusion of themes	
Overall discussion at the end summarising findings	
Reappraisal of research questions	

References

Cottrell, S. (2017) *Critical thinking skills: Effective analysis, argument and reflection.* 3rd edn. London: Plagrave.

Ennis, R. H. (2011) *The nature of critical thinking: An outline of critical thinking dispositions and abilities.* Available at: https://education.illinois.edu/docs/default-source/faculty-documents/robert-ennis/thenatureofcriticalthinking_51711_000.pdf.

Moon, J. (2007) *Critical thinking: An exploration of theory and practice.* London: Routledge.

Samuels, P. C. (2021) Dissertations in 20 steps – a platonic discussion. Technical report. *ResearchGate.* Available at: www.researchgate.net/publication/3496406 39_Dissertations_in_20_Steps_-_a_Platonic_Discussion.

10   Conceptual frameworks

Introduction

A conceptual framework is more specific to your context than a theoretical framework. It summarises the findings of your literature review and presents them in the form of a diagram. This diagram should represent your evaluation of how the most important concepts relating to your study interconnect. For a more detailed discussion on the distinction between conceptual frameworks and theoretical frameworks, please refer to Varpio et al.'s (2020) useful paper.

Conceptual frameworks are generally an optional extra in proposals. If you are planning to collect primary data, they can form a useful visual bridge between the findings of your literature review and the design of your data collection instrument.

General advice

The best place to put a conceptual framework is either towards the end of your literature review or near the start of your methodology/method section.

Conceptual frameworks come in two main forms:

- **Process diagrams** which connect concepts with arrows
- **Tree diagrams** which split an overall concept into areas and sub-areas

There is no hard and fast rule about how to present a conceptual framework. It is best to **read** relevant research articles relating to your own study and get an idea on an appropriate format from any of these which contain a conceptual framework.

However, if you are planning to carry out quantitative research, it is important to bear in mind that conceptual frameworks contain concepts which may not be measurable. It is only once you have discussed how you plan to measure these concepts in your methodology/method section, and

DOI: 10.4324/9781003285137-14

whether this is **valid** and **reliable**, that you should present a quantitative model or hypotheses based on them.

Examples

The only conceptual framework presented in one of the example proposals is the model cited at the end of Tappasiya's introduction which is shown in Figure 10.1.

This model is in the form of a process diagram with purchase intentions depending upon other concepts as indicated by the arrows. It has been taken from a paper published by other researchers. Whilst it is good that Tappasiya's conceptual model was informed by someone else's work, it would have been better if she had **adapted** or **applied** this to her context based on the findings of her literature review. The different concepts represented in this diagram could then be measured either by closed questions in a questionnaire or from other secondary sources of information.

Tamvada (2020) has developed a conceptual framework for the relationship between different elements of corporate social responsibility as shown in Figure 10.2.

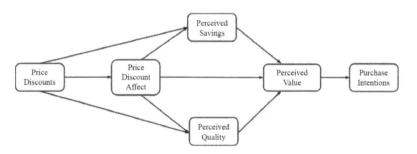

Figure 10.1 Conceptual model in Tappasiya's proposal
Source: (Lee and Chen-Yu, 2018: 5)

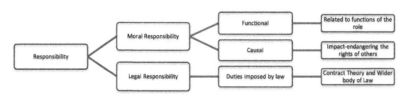

Figure 10.2 Conceptual framework for the relationship between different elements of corporate social responsibility
Source: (Tamvada, 2020: 7)

Her framework is in the form of a tree diagram. There are two main areas of responsibility, one of which is split into two sub-areas. Each of these areas could be translated into one or more questions in a data collection instrument, such as an interview or a questionnaire.

Exercise

Create a diagram which describes the relationship between the main concepts relevant to your chosen topic. How does this compare with conceptual frameworks in studies similar to your own?

References

Lee, J. E. and Chen-Yu, J. H. (2018) Effects of price discount on consumers' perceptions of savings, quality, and value for apparel products: Mediating effect of price discount affect. *Fashion and Textiles*, 5(1), pp. 1–21.

Tamvada, M. (2020) Corporate social responsibility and accountability: A new theoretical foundation for regulating CSR. *International Journal of Corporate Social Responsibility*, 5(1), pp. 1–14.

Varpio, L., Paradis, E., Uijtdehaage, S. and Young, M. (2020) The distinctions between theory, theoretical framework, and conceptual framework. *Academic Medicine*, 95(7), pp. 989–994.

11 Writing your methodology/ method section

Introduction: why the name confusion?

Methodology and method go together. **Methodology** refers to **theory** of how research should be undertaken, including its **philosophical** underpinnings, the **approach** to generating new knowledge and the **strategy** used to obtain suitable data. **Method** refers to the techniques and procedures used to **collect** and **analyse data**. Unfortunately there is no suitable single word which refers to them both at the same time.

Methodology/method sections in proposals are often poorly written. This is mainly due to misunderstandings about the technical terms they involve or a failure to understand what the target audience is expecting to read. This is another long chapter as there are many issues that need to be explained, which you might find unfamiliar.

Methodology and method can be viewed as concentric layers as shown in Figure 11.1.

Purpose and argumentation style

The purpose of a methodology/method section in a proposal is to **present a credible plan** for the choices you intend to implement in your research. This means the style of argumentation should be single argument/opinion rather than discursive.

There is a temptation in a methodology/method section to explain the meaning of different basic concepts. This should not be your emphasis as you may assume that your reader already understands them. However, what they do not know is **what methodology/method you have chosen, why you believe it is appropriate in your context** and **how you intend to implement it**. The choices you make need to be **consistent** and **presented in a logical order**. The length of your methodology/method section should be **about 25% of your total wordcount**.

DOI: 10.4324/9781003285137-15

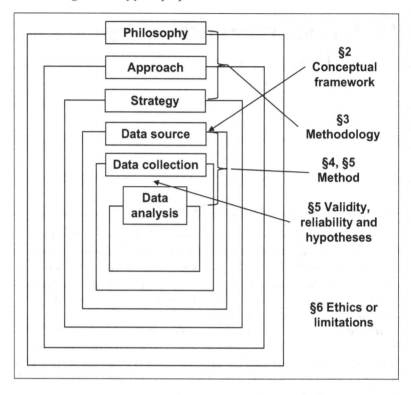

Figure 11.1 Overview of the main elements of methodology and method
Source: Adapted from (Saunders et al., 2019: 130)

Structure

The recommended structure of a methodology/method section is:

§1 Introduction
§2 Conceptual framework
§3 Methodology (including philosophy, approach and strategy)
§4 Data collection
§5 Data analysis
§6 Ethics or limitations

The introduction should mainly explain how the rest of your section has been organised.

For conceptual frameworks, please refer to the previous chapter. For longer proposals the methodology subsection can be subdivided further into philosophy, approach and strategy. For shorter proposals, you may need to choose between presenting a conceptual framework and details about your philosophical choice.

The other parts of this structure are described in the following sections below.

Philosophy

A philosophy is **a theoretical way of viewing research and the new knowledge it constructs**. According to Saunders et al. (2019: 144–145), there are five main philosophies relevant to business contexts:

Positivism: This is the philosophy associated with the **scientific method**; it involves observable facts; the researcher remains objective, neutral and detached from the research; it is suitable for quantitative research.

Interpretivism: The focus of this philosophy is on **narratives, perceptions** and **interpretations**; the researcher is seen as part of research, and needs to be able to articulate how their identity may have affected their interpretations (known as being **reflexive**); this is the standard philosophy for qualitative research.

Critical realism: In this philosophy, knowledge is viewed as being **relative** and **socially constructed**; the researcher needs to acknowledge their identity, remain as objective as possible and try to minimize bias.

Postmodernism: This philosophy focuses on **oppressed and repressed meanings**; the researcher is usually embedded within the power relationships so needs to be reflexive; this is a useful perspective when investigating gender issues, ethnic minorities, disabilities or potential mistreatment of employees.

Pragmatism: The emphasis of this philosophy is on **practical meanings, problem solving** and **relevance** to enable successful action; it is initiated by researcher's doubts and beliefs and also requires reflexivity; it is useful when attempting to improve a process in a working environment or solve a problem in a business context.

As already mentioned above, with a concise proposal, you may need to choose between explaining your choice of philosophy and including a conceptual framework.

Approach

Approach refers to the **way in which new knowledge is generated**. There are three main approaches:

Deductive: the use of data to decide whether a pre-existing theory or hypothesis is true or false; this is associated with quantitative research.

Inductive: the process of establishing new knowledge from collected data; this is associated with qualitative research.

Abductive: a process of moving back and forth between deduction and induction, for example, using interviews to establish the questions to be included in a closed questionnaire; this approach is associated with mixed methods research where two techniques are used one after the other.

For more information, please refer to (Saunders et al., 2019: 152–158).

Strategy

Your strategy is your **systematic means of obtaining data** in order to achieve your objectives or answer your research questions. There are seven main research strategies. I will start by exploring the most common business research strategies in more depth:

Strategy 1: Surveys

A survey is a **systematic collection of information from a sample of people from a larger population**. In business research this often refers to a company's employees or consumers. There are three main types of data collection instrument for carrying out a survey:

- A **questionnaire** where the same written questions are given out asynchronously
- **Interviews** where individuals are asked the same or similar questions synchronously
- **Focus groups** where a group of six to ten people meet together to collectively explore a research issue

With a survey it is important to state what your **population** is and how you are **sampling** it. This is the process of identifying your data source. There are two main kinds of sampling:

- **Random**: which involves having access to all individuals in your population and choosing a sample from them using a randomized process
- **Non-random**: where you select sample using some other means

Examples

Mollie is planning to conduct a survey. In her *Theory and Strategy* subsection, she states:

> *The questionnaire will be offered to people over the age of 18 who have an interest in the current situation regarding the government taxes and the effect that coronavirus has had on the taxation situation in the past year.*

The population for her survey sounds rather vague. Presumably it refers to any adult in the UK who is not considered vulnerable. Her description of them having an interest in certain issues sounds difficult for her to establish before approaching them unless she has a strategy involving some kind of interest group, such as via social media.

Vague data source choices lead to vague findings which are of little value.

Thomas is planning to conduct two separate surveys. In his *Data Collection* subsection, he states:

> *Questionnaires and semi-structured interviews will be used to collect ethnographic data from employees working for the research's case study business, Kyocera Document Solutions Europe, a Japanese business based in the Netherlands. Managers and employees alike from both European and Japanese nationalities will be researched within this business to compare the attitudes, behaviours and beliefs of different national cultures and the cultural issues that arise from the cooperation of these co-workers in the workplace.*

His statement is much more specific as it relates to managers and employees within a certain international organisation. However, Thomas was eventually unable to undertake this primary data collection and later switched to secondary data collection only.

Neither Thomas nor Mollie explained whether their sampling was random or non-random. As Mollie's population is so vague, she probably could only adopt a non-random sampling approach, such as **purposive sampling** (where you choose the sample) or **snowball sampling** (where you start with people you can identify as relevant then ask them for more contacts).

From these two examples we observe that it is important to **be specific about your population** for a survey, but you also need to **do some informal groundwork** before deciding to carry out a survey so that you can be confident that you will be able to collect the data that you are hoping to.

Sample size recommendations for surveys

For undergraduate and master's research projects it is recommended that you should aim to collect **between 50 and 100 questionnaires**, carry out between **six and ten interviews**, or organise **two focus groups** containing six to ten members.

Questionnaires tend to mainly have closed questions which lead to quantitative analysis. Quantitative analysis works best when you compare groups or answers to different questions. In order to detect differences and relationships you will need a reasonably large sample. There are no hard and fast rules about this, but quantitative analysis becomes increasingly difficult and less useful with smaller sample sizes. On the other hand, it is often difficult to obtain a large sample size in the short time period of undergraduate or master's level research.

Even if you include some open-ended questions, it is often difficult to get your respondents to reply in depth. Whilst online or email questionnaire require less resources to administer, the main challenge is often **low response rates** and the possibility of **bias** (your sample not reflecting the views of the whole population). You therefore need to distribute more questionnaires than you expect to receive back, and have a strategy to maximise your response rate. This should be discussed in your proposal.

Interviews and focus groups lead to the collection of textual data which will require a qualitative analysis technique. It is important to have a sufficiently large sample to allow some variation between individuals or groups, but not too much data so that your analysis can focus on **depth of interpretation** rather than description.

Strategy 2: Case studies

A case study is a **systematic attempt to account for the complexity and depth of one or more cases**. In business research the cases usually refer to one or more business organisations. It is recommended that you only research a single case or a comparison between two cases which has a clear rationale behind their choices.

It is sometimes difficult to decide whether to frame a research project as a survey or as a case study. The population associated with a survey might be staff employed in a single organisation which might also lend itself to a case study. However, the main distinction between a survey and a case study is that case studies seek to look at a context from the viewpoint of **multiple stakeholders**, for example employees, managers, customers, shareholders and regulatory authorities. Therefore, case studies might include surveys as part of their strategy.

For more information, please refer to (Farquhar, 2012).

Strategy 3: Ethnography

Ethnography is the **systematic study of people and cultures**. In business research this usually refers to business cultures, such as those experienced by a researcher who is on a work placement, such as an employee, or intern or a charity worker.

Strategy 4: Secondary data

Secondary data is the **systematic search, selection and analysis of data collected by others**. This is either **raw data** which you analyse yourself or **published research articles** for which you conduct a secondary analysis, known as a systematic review.

Other less common strategies

There are three other relevant strategies which are less common in a business research context.

Strategy 5: Action research: A systematic, reflective and cooperative process of progressive problem solving; in business research this involves collaboration with other stakeholders such as fellow employees in an organisation; this might be appropriate during or after a work placement if you already have an idea of some process which could be improved.

Strategy 6: Experiments: An orderly procedure carried out to test a hypothesis. Experiments are more common in scientific contexts.

Strategy 7: Grounded theory: A systematic approach to analyse, explain and theorise everyday experiences. This strategy is different from the grounded theory approach to analysing qualitative data as it focuses on collecting sufficient data for a new theory about a phenomenon to be generated. It is only recommended for more advanced studies, such as doctorates.

Data collection

Once you have explained your methodology you should describe your data collection plans. There are four main **primary data collection** techniques in a business context:

- **Questionnaires** – a collection of written questions, usually responded to at a different time to when they are asked (**asynchronously**) – see (Frazer and Lawley, 2000; Oppenheim, 2000). The questions can either be **open** or **closed**. Open questions lead to textual data. Closed questions lead to categorical or numerical data.
- **Interviews** – a series of structured question-based live meetings with one person at a time. The recommended style is a **semi-structured interview** in which the interviewer prepares a series of questions in advance but allows the respondent to give additional information, provided that it is still viewed as relevant to their overall research aim – see (Rubin and Rubin, 2005).
- **Focus groups** – a collective approach ideally by a group of six to ten people, to discuss and solve a specific issue or problem – see (Krueger and Casey, 2014).
- **Observations** – a systematic personal approach to data collection involving prolonged engagement in a social setting, recording your observations using predefined notations, improvisations to develop a full understanding, and paying attention in a standard way – see (Cohen and Crabtree, 2006)

For each technique you choose you should explain **what** it is, **why** you have chosen it, and **how** you are planning to implement it. With questionnaires, interviews and focus groups, the choice of questions could be linked to the findings of your literature review through a conceptual framework. In addition, if you are planning to undertake a questionnaire, you should explain and justify your choice of format, such as paper-based, email or online.

For secondary data collection you should explain your sources of data and your selection methods.

Example

Kate specifies her sources of secondary data in her *Data collection* subsection:

> *The majority of data will be collected on the six member countries of the EAC. Data concerning changes in international trade will be collected from the World Trade Organisation (WTO), EAC archives and the respective nations' government archives. Data concerning*

*changes in Gross Domestic Product (GDP) and Foreign Direct Invest-
ment (FDI) over time will be obtained from Our World in Data and the
World Bank.*

Kate's paragraph provides specific information on **where** she is planning to
obtain her data and **what** data she intends to obtain from each data source.
However, it could have been improved in the following ways:

- Rather than stating data sources, it would have been better if she had
  used a word such as "**including**" to indicate specific choices whilst
  leaving room for possible future changes
- Whilst the specific data sources sound authoritative, some simple descrip-
  tions could have been added to indicate **why** they are perceived as being
  authoritative. For example, an argument could have been provided indicating that the World Trade Organisation is the main recognised world
  authority on international trade which keeps accurate, open and accessible
  records on individual countries.
- A **citation** should be given for each data set.

Validity, reliability and hypotheses

With quantitative data, it is also often important to discuss the **measurement** of your concepts and how this might lead to testing your theory:

- Measurements are **valid** if they measure what they are supposed to
  measure.
- Measurements are **reliable** if the same or similar results are obtained
  when they are re-measured, or a group of questions can be shown to
  measure the same thing.
- A **hypothesis** is a statement about the **relationship between measurable
  quantities**. These may follow on from the relationship between concepts
  in your conceptual framework. **Statistical testing** is the quantitative data
  analysis process leading to the acceptance or rejection of a hypothesis.

Data analysis

Data analysis will depend on the **type** of data you intend to collect:

- Numerical and categorical data will lead to **quantitative analysis**
- Textual data will lead to **qualitative analysis**
- A combination of the two will lead to **mixed methods analysis**

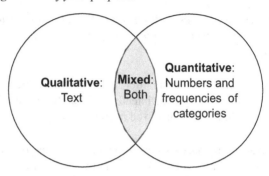

Figure 11.2 Relationship between data types and data analysis

This is illustrated in Figure 11.2.

Quantitative analysis

This can broadly be divided into descriptive analysis and statistical testing:

- **Descriptive analysis** involves the presentation of **tables, charts** and summaries of data sets, known as **summary statistics**, for example, means and standard deviations. You should choose an appropriate representation of your data, provide a narrative to go with it and an informal interpretation of its meaning. You should aim for your choice of tables and charts to represent relationships between your concepts rather than just a single concept. To this end, representation such as **multi series tables, percentage frequency bar charts** and **scatter plots** are useful.
- **Statistical testing** is the process of making a decision about a hypothesis you have stated in advance. There are many different types of statistical testing depending on the design of your study, including:

    - Tests which compare a measured quantity against different groups
    - Tests which compare one measured quantity against another
    - Tests which assume data comes from a predetermined distribution
    - Tests which do not make this assumption

For more information, please refer to (Samuels, 2020).

Qualitative analysis

If qualitative data is very brief, which is typical of answers to open ended questions in a questionnaire, then a frequency-based approach can be adopted. This often involves counting the frequency of words or synonyms.

For longer pieces of text, **qualitative content analysis** should be used. This can be conceptualised in three stages:

- **Primary analysis**: informal notes made when reading transcripts, similar to the process of **critical reading** – see (Seyler, 2014: Chapter 1).
- **Category formation**: this is a more formal process involving identifying types of information in transcripts, known as **categories**, and giving them a name. Categories may then be combined together into **themes**. In order for the research to be inductive, the names of the categories and themes should be new and therefore different from the concepts identified in your literature review and conceptual framework.
- **Theory generation** and **comparative analysis**. This is an optional final stage in which a theory is generated which explains how a phenomenon works across different people or situations.

For general information on qualitative data analysis, please refer to (Saunders et al., 2019: 636–705; Woods, 2013). For business specific advice, please see (van den Berg and Struwig, 2017).

Ideally, qualitative analysis should be undertaken from a **theoretical perspective**, such as **grounded theory** (O'Reilly et al., 2012). For general information on theory-based qualitative data analysis, see (Schutt, 2012).

Ethics

You might also wish to discuss ethical issues towards the end of your methodology/method section. These include:

- Measures to protect participants and researchers from potential harm
- Right of participants to withdraw
- Collection of appropriate data
- Measures to protect the identity of participants, such as anonymisation
- Protection of stored data

Example

Thomas provides a brief ethical statement about protecting the anonymity of his participants towards the end of his methodology/method section:

> *The qualitative data achieved through both the semi-structured interviews and questionnaires about employees' experiences with cross-cultural conflicts at the workplace will be analysed and interpreted by the author of this study, who will maintain questionnaire participant anonymity*

throughout to reduce researcher bias. Additionally, in analysis, interviewee names will be redacted by the author to protect anonymity.

Limitations

You might also wish to discuss potential limitations to your research at the end of this section, such as non-random sample selection, low response rates to online questionnaires, potential difficulties in organising interviews or focus groups and contingency plans you might adopt to ensure you obtain a sufficient amount of data.

Common mistakes

- **Focusing too much on what different stages and choices of methodology/ method mean rather than focusing on your choices and your reasons for them**. There is no need to try to educate your reader about things they already understand.
- **Misusing the generic descriptors quantitative and qualitative to refer to your research in general, vague terms**. It is probably better to avoid these descriptors in this section, or only use them very sparingly.
- **Only explaining your choices rather than the reasons for them or how they are going to be implemented**. For example, with a choice of a questionnaire, it is important to know **why** this data collection method has been preferred to others, **how** the question design will relate to the findings of the literature review, **what** the population and sampling approach will be, and **what** format it will take (e.g. paper-based or online).
- **Over-structuring your section**. For example, explaining your choice of **research design** often overlaps with other methodology subsections introduced above and is not recommended. Also, nearly all undergraduate and master's research is cross-sectional (i.e. data is collected over a single short time period) so discussions about **time horizon** are usually irrelevant and have been omitted above.
- **Making inconsistent choices**, such as an inductive approach and a closed form of data collection.
- **Only citing a single reference**, such as (Saunders et al., 2019). You need to read about methodology and method more widely and cite several authors, such as some of those recommended in this chapter.
- **Including too much critical discussion**. Your focus should be on presenting your plan for data collection and analysis within your methodological context.

Evaluating methodology/method sections: DECJAD

The mnemonic **DECJAD** stands for:

- **D**escribe – does the subsection explain briefly what the subsection means?
- **E**vidence – does the subsection contain evidence to back up the claims made?
- **C**hoice – does the subsection clearly explain the choices made?
- **J**ustify – are the choices justified with a persuasive argument?
- **A**pply – are the choices made applied to the context?
- **D**iscuss – does the subsection include some limited discussion towards the end?

You should not expect a yes answer for each question for each subsection as the choice of writing will be selective. However, DECJAD can help you to understand and evaluate what kinds of writing each subsection contains.

Example

Kate's methodology/method section have been evaluated in Table 11.1.

Kate's methodology/method section contains subsections on *Methodology*, *Data collection* and *Data analysis*. Her *Methodology* subsection covers her philosophy and approach. Her strategy choice of secondary data is provided under her Data collection subsection. However, she also mentions it being a case study, which is probably inappropriate as she is not investigating the East African Community in depth or from multiple perspectives.

Overall, Kate clearly explains her choices and mostly provides a persuasive justification for them based on her context. However, the main weakness in her section is her lack of evidence to back up her choices. For example, whilst there is no need for her to explain what a philosophy is, it would have been useful if she had provided a brief definition of her chosen pragmatic

Table 11.1 Evaluation of Kate's methodology/method section

Subsection	Describe	Evidence	Choice	Justify	Apply	Discuss
Philosophy	✗	✗	✓	✓	✓	✗
Approach	✗	✗	✓	✓	✓	✗
Strategy	✗	✗	✓	✓	✓	✗
Data collection	✗	✗	✓	✓	✓	✗
Data analysis	✗	✗	✓	✗	✓	✗

Table 11.2 DECJAD checklist

Subsection	Describe	Evidence	Choice	Justify	Apply	Discuss
Philosophy						
Approach						
Strategy						
Data collection						
Data analysis						

philosophy and backed this up with a citation. Her lack of discussion in each subsection is less important and would not have been expected in a concise methodology/method section such as this.

Exercise

Evaluate the subsections of your draft methodology and methods using DECJAD using the checklist in Table 11.2.

Finally, reflect on your evaluation of your draft section in the light of Kate's example above so that you have an idea of how to improve it.

References

Cohen, D. and Crabtree, B. (2006) Observation. In *Qualitative research guidelines project*. Princeton, NJ: Robert Wood Johnson Foundation. Available at: www.qualres.org/HomeObse-3594.html.

Farquhar, J. D. (2012) *Case study research for business*. London: SAGE.

Frazer, L. and Lawley, M. (2000) *Questionnaire design and administration: A practical guide*. Chichester: Wiley.

Krueger, R. A. and Casey, M. A. (2014) *Focus groups: A practical guide for applied research*. 5th edn. London: SAGE.

Oppenheim, A. N. (2000) *Questionnaire design, interviewing and attitude measurement*. New edn. London: Continuum.

O'Reilly, K., Paper, D. and Marx, S. (2012) Demystifying grounded theory for business research. *Organizational Research Methods*, 15(2), pp. 247–262.

Rubin, H. and Rubin, I. (2005) *Qualitative interviewing: The art of hearing data*. 2nd edn. London: SAGE.

Samuels, P. C. (2020) *A really simple guide to quantitative data analysis*. Available at: www.researchgate.net/publication/340838762_A_Really_Simple_Guide_to_Quantitative_Data_Analysis.

Saunders, M., Lewis, P. and Thornhill, A. (2019) *Research methods for business students*. 8th edn. Harlow: Pearson.

Schutt, R. K. (2012) Qualitative data analysis. In R. K. Schutt, ed. *Investigating the social world*. 7th edn. London: SAGE [pdf]. Available at: www.sagepub.com/sites/default/files/upmbinaries/43454_10.pdf.

Seyler, D. (2014) *Read, reason, write: An argument text and reader*. 11th edn. New York: McGraw-Hill Education.

van den Berg, A. and Struwig, M. (2017) Guidelines for researchers using an adapted consensual qualitative research approach in management research. *Electronic Journal of Business Research Methods*, 15(2), pp. 109–119. Available at: https://academic-publishing.org/index.php/ejbrm/article/download/1361/1324.

Woods, P. (2013) *Qualitative research*. The Open University. Available at: www.open.edu/openlearnworks/mod/resource/view.php?id=5 1902.

12 Producing a schedule

Gantt charts

A final common section in the main body of a proposal is a schedule of tasks. The recommended way of representing this is with a **Gantt chart**. This has one row for each task and the period for doing the research project is split up equally into columns. The time span over which each task is active is then shown by filled cells in its respective row.

Example

An example of a Gantt chart is shown in Figure 12.1.

Some points to note about this example Gantt chart are:

• There is a **manageable number of tasks** which split the research project up in sufficient detail. It is recommended that you have between ten and 20 tasks.
• Each task is **output orientated** – you can tell when it is complete as it relates to a specific output.
• There are a **manageable number of columns**. This example is for a master's dissertation which is undertaken over a single semester, so the columns are weeks. For two-semester dissertations you might use fortnights or half-month columns. For a doctorate you might use two-month columns. You should aim for between 12 and 25 columns.
• Several tasks are being conducted in **parallel** at different times.
• There are **dependencies** between some of the tasks; for example, the data cannot be analysed until data collection has started, and this cannot start until the research instrument has been designed and the ethics request has been approved.
• There is a one-week **contingency** at the end in case there is a delay in the completion of some of the tasks.

DOI: 10.4324/9781003285137-16

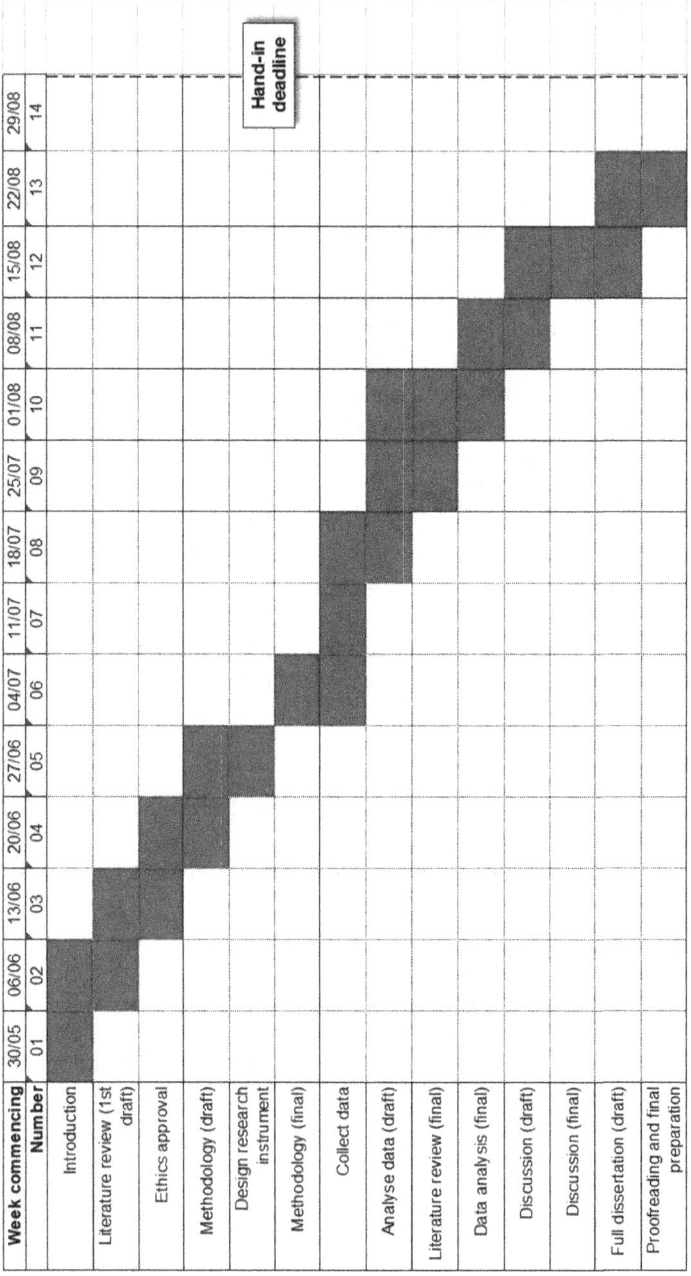

Week commencing	30/05	06/06	13/06	20/06	27/06	04/07	11/07	18/07	25/07	01/08	08/08	15/08	22/08	29/08
Number	01	02	03	04	05	06	07	08	09	10	11	12	13	14
Introduction	▓													
Literature review (1st draft)		▓	▓											
Ethics approval			▓	▓										
Methodology (draft)				▓	▓									
Design research instrument					▓									
Methodology (final)						▓								
Collect data						▓	▓							
Analyse data (draft)								▓	▓					
Literature review (final)								▓						
Data analysis (final)										▓	▓			
Discussion (draft)											▓	▓		
Discussion (final)												▓		
Full dissertation (draft)												▓	▓	
Proofreading and final preparation													▓	

Hand-in deadline

Figure 12.1 Example Gantt chart

I recommend that you use a simple spreadsheet package, such as Excel, to create your Gantt chart rather than a more sophisticated project management package. All you need to do is colour the cells relating to the time periods over which the tasks are scheduled to be active.

Research phases

In addition to providing tasks, it might also be useful to add **research phases** to your chart. A common characterisation of these is:

*   **Conceptual** – coming up with an initial idea, formulating it and writing a proposal – this might be left out from a Gantt chart if you are submitting it with your proposal as it will already have completed
*   **Critical** – carrying out your main literature review, writing your methodology chapter, obtaining ethics approval, and designing your data collection instrument
*   **Action** – collecting your data and preparing it for analysis
*   **Analysis** – analysing your data and writing up your findings
*   **Creative** – writing your discussion, conclusions and putting your final report together

These phases should be viewed as **overlapping**; for example, you may start the critical phase before you complete the conceptual phase.

Example

Kate has provided research phases at the bottom of her Gantt chart as shown in Figure 12.2.

Her choice of phases and associated tasks seems to make a lot of sense.

Accompanying narrative

In addition to providing a Gantt chart, you should write a short narrative explaining your chart. This can describe your tasks, explain why they are in the sequence and of the length shown, then discuss possible issues relating to managing your research project.

Example

Mollie has written two paragraphs to accompany her Gantt chart:

> *In the Gantt chart that I have created I have identified the main tasks that I am aiming to do week by week, along with some of the more important*

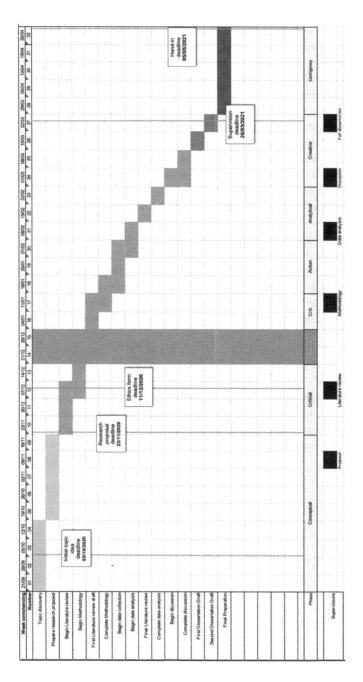

Figure 12.2 Kate's Gantt chart

tasks, such as deadlines and supervisor meetings. On my chart the date is displayed across the top, and then there are different tasks listed down the left-hand side. The boxes that I have marked in blue are the tasks of high importance, which include supervisor meetings and deadlines for the proposal hand in and the completed research project hand in. The rest of the chart is coloured in pink and shows weekly tasks that I intend to complete in order to get my research project handed in on time.

This chart shows the plan that I am going to follow throughout the course of this project, and has some time left over at the end in case any issues are encountered throughout the process. This will make sure that I don't run out of time to complete the project. If any problems arise whilst I am working towards completing my research project, then at least I have left enough time to correct my work before I have to hand it in.

Whilst her first paragraph explains the meaning of her chart, she could have assumed some of this and focused more on explaining what the key tasks or phases were in her research project. Her second paragraph justifies her contingency plan of extra time at the end and is rather repetitive. She could also have explored other potential difficulties with managing her project, such as critical dependencies or possible non-availability of resources at the scheduled times.

Exercise

Use a spreadsheet package to create a draft Gantt chart like the example above that represents the tasks in your research project, then draft an accompanying narrative that explains it and discusses potential problems that you might encounter and how you plan to manage them.

13 Referencing

Introduction

Referencing is the process of giving attribution to external sources and presented data (tables and charts) within your proposal. Attributing external sources commonly involves **citing** in the main body of the text followed by a reference list at the end. In social sciences this often means using an **alphabetical style** referencing system, such as Harvard or APA. This means the references in the list should be given in the alphabetical order of the author(s) or institutions who created them.

You should be given specific guidance on how to reference at your institution. For general principles on referencing, please refer to (Pears and Shields, 2022) and its associated website (www.citethemrightonline.com/). For additional guidance on some common referencing systems, please refer to the referencing resources in the Purdue Online Writing Lab (https://owl. purdue.edu/owl/research_and_citation/resources.html).

Citing

With alphabetical referencing systems, the author's surname is used in the citation. This can be done at the end of a sentence by putting the name and the year of the publication in a bracket, which is known as an **indirect citation**. Alternatively, the author's name can be put in a sentence and just the year is put in a bracket, which is known as a **direct citation**. Generally, direct citations are preferred as they make the writing appear more personal and allow you to provide a more accurate citation. However, the downside is that they use more words.

There are also rules about sources with **multiple authors**, which depend on the system being used, and how to present **quotations** (word-for-word citations).

DOI: 10.4324/9781003285137-17

Examples

The second half of Kate's opening paragraph illustrates these issues:

> *While such agreements originally focused on trade integration,*
> *RIAs have become multidimensional and may incorporate other*
> *common institutions such as a monetary union or shared political*
> *establishments (Katembo, 2008). The most successful example of*
> *an RIA would be the European Union (EU) which has achieved "a*
> *process in which units move from a condition of total or partial iso-*
> *lation towards a complete or partial unification" (p. 5), which De*
> *Lombaerde and Van Langenhove's (2005) describe to be the mea-*
> *sure of integration.*

* (*Katembo, 2008*) is an indirect citation. This has been done correctly.
* *which De Lombaerde and Van Langenhove's (2005) describe* . . . is a
  direct citation with two authors. The only problem with this is the *'s*
  after *Langenhove*, which appears inappropriate.
* *"a process in which units move from a condition of total or partial*
  isolation towards a complete or partial unification" (p. 5) is a quotation.
  It is correctly followed by a page number, but it is unclear which citation
  this quotation relates to.

Mollie has attempted a direct quote citation with several authors in her literature review:

> *Collier, R et al, page 794, stated that "In the first phase, while the*
> *lockdown is in place and countries are experiencing an acute overall*
> *disruption, tax measures can help mitigate the impact of the crisis by*
> *providing businesses and households with cash flow in order to avoid a*
> *complete collapse of the economy . . .".*

Et al. means *and others* and is the correct way to cite a source with
more than two authors in Mollie's referencing system. However, she has
incorrectly included an initial and left out the year. She should also have
page number after a colon without the word "Page". Her quote itself is
also rather long, especially for a proposal. Quotes should generally be
kept to about **30 words or one sentence maximum**. Longer passages
should be summarised.

Mollie should have cited this quote using:

> *Collier et al. (2020: 794), stated that, ". . ."*

Tables and figures

Tables and figures should be labelled consistently and referred to in the text before they are presented. If they contain data from an external source, this should be acknowledged including the page number, where it exists.

Examples

Kate has included a figure in her *Introduction* section which she labelled like this:

> Figure 1.0 *Members of the East African Community (EAC) with their respective 2019 GDP figures (in Billions).*
> *Source: World Bank Data 2020.*

- Kate has labelled her figure correctly, and also provided the source document from which it was obtained
- However, she has not referred to this figure in her text before she presented it
- It would be better if her figure was larger so that the text could be read more easily, and it was centred in the middle of the page
- The source citation should be in brackets and include the page number of the figure (if one exists)

Later on, in her *Literature Review*, Kate presents a table which she has labelled like this:

> Table 1.1 *Global trade: exports, 2015–2018 (percentage growth).*
> *Source: EAC Trade and Investment Report 2018.*

- Again, she has labelled the table correctly and provided the source citation
- But again, there is no reference to Table 1.1 in the text before she presented this table
- And again, the source citation should contain the page number and be presented in a bracket

Reference lists

With in-text citation styles of referencing, a reference list should be provided at the end of the proposal which includes all the sources cited in the text. With alphabetical in-text style systems, these should be presented in alphabetical order of the first author. Only one reference should be provided for each source even if it has been cited several times. The sources should not be split up according to the type of publication.

Each type of citation (for example, journal articles, books and electronic reports) has a different citation style, but they have common features. You should not simply cut and paste citations of your cited sources from someone else's work as these may not conform to your institution's style. However, you can use these as the basis for creating your own references. Google Scholar (https://scholar.google.co.uk/) also has a *double-quote* button which you can use to obtain citation details in standard formats.

Examples

Kate has included a reference in her reference list as follows:
De Lombaerde, P. and Van Langenhove, L., 2005. Indicators of regional integration: Methodological issues.

Putting the authors' names, year and title into Google Scholar, I managed to identify this publication. It is also freely available as a PDF – see Figure 13.1.

Opening the PDF it became clear that this was a technical report. Some of the details in Kate's reference were missing. As the PDF was not available from an official site the correct way to reference this publication at Kate's institution would be for a paper version as follows:

De Lombaerde, P. and Van Langenhove, L. (2005) *Indicators of Regional Integration: Methodological issues*. IIIS Discussion Paper No. 64. Dublin: Institute for International Integration Studies.

Figure 13.1 Google Scholar output after searching for Kate's source publication
Source: (Google, 2022)

In Mollie's reference list there is the following entry:

Collier, R. Pirlot, A. Vella, J. (2020) 'Covid-19 and Fiscal Policies: Tax Policy and the COVID-19 Crisis, Volume 48 (Issue 8), Page 794.

She has mistakenly not referred to a whole article, but only the page from which she has taken a quote. The journal title was also missing. Again, by using Google Scholar, I was able to check this reference and discovered that that author names and the issue number were also incorrect. She should have referenced this journal article at her institution like this:

Vella, J. and Collier, R. (2020) COVID-19 and Fiscal Policies: Tax Policy and the COVID-19 Crisis. *Intertax*, 48(8/9), pp. 794–804.

Thomas included the reference to a book in his reference list as follows:

Adler, N.J. (2002) International Dimensions of Organizational Behavior, 4th edn.

This was nearly correct for his institution. The only issues were the lack of a publisher, which I was able to find by using Google Books (https://books.google.com/), a place of publication, which I found by Googling the publisher's name, and not putting the title in italics. The correct way for Thomas to cite this book at his institution would be:

Adler, N. J. (2002) *International Dimensions of Organizational Behavior*, 4th edn. Cincinnati OH: South-Western.

Tappasiya generated her reference list automatically using the Harvard style in the Word References function. Unfortunately, she was not aware that there are many different variants of Harvard, so the version she used was not completely correct for her institution. One of the references she generated was for a website:

Corcoran, D., 2018. *Three Customer Experience Lessons From Amazon.* [Online]
Available at: https://thefinancialbrand.com/70509/banking-customer-experience-cx-lessons-amazon/
[Accessed 31 August 2020].

For her institution, the year should have been in brackets, the word [Online] should be omitted, the URL link should work, and the reference should be displayed on a single line like this:

Corcoran, D. (2018) *Three Customer Experience Lessons from Amazon.* Available at: https://thefinancialbrand.com/70509/banking-customer-experience-cx-lessons-amazon/ [Accessed 31 August 2020].

Otherwise, her reference was correct.

References

Google (2022) *Google Scholar UK search result for De Lombaerde Van Langenhove 2005 Indicators of regional integration: Methodological issues.* Available at: https://scholar.google.co.uk/scholar?hl=en&as_sdt=0%2C5&q=De+Lombaerde+Van+Langenhove+2005+Indicators+of+regional+integration%3A+Methodological+issues&btnG=.
Pears, R. and Shields, G. (2022) *Cite them right.* 12th edn. London: Bloomsbury Academic.

Part Four

Beyond your proposal

Introduction

Now that we have covered everything involved in deciding on, researching and writing your proposal, the remainder of this book provides three chapters containing concise information on your next steps as a dissertation research student. There are many other resources written on these subjects, which no doubt you will be accessing, but these chapters provide some initial guidance and some pointers of where to look for more information.

Chapter 14 covers planning and managing your research, including stress management. Chapter 15 focuses on your relationship with your supervisor and how to get the most out of it. Finally Chapter 16 introduces the tasks you will be undertaking after submitting your proposal, commonly referred to as the **critical phase** of doing a dissertation (see the *Research phases* section of Chapter 12).

DOI: 10.4324/9781003285137-18

14 Time and stress management

Time management

General principles

Here are some general time management tips, some of which are based on the advice available from Coaching Positive Performance (2018):

- Try to address and **resolve any emotional or social distractions** before you try to start working as these can affect your ability to concentrate. You will need to spend some time investing in developing effective working relationships with those around you.
- Use critical thinking to **identify and evaluate** the **tasks** you need to complete; write them down and assess their relative levels of **urgency** and **importance**. For example, you could write them on post-it notes and place them on a grid – see Figure 14.1. Make sure you leave enough time for important tasks which are less urgent (Priority 2) as these can often bite you if you focus too much on urgent tasks which are less important (Priority 3).
- Based on your task list and evaluation, and the amount of time you have available, **choose the right task to do first** then **focus** on it; you will have a better overall outcome if you focus on and spend enough time doing high priority tasks well.
- It is good to be aware of your own self-motivation and use this to improve your performance. For example, do you enjoy finishing tasks? Do you like to keep your information tidy? Would a picture help you to get your thoughts down on paper before focusing on a writing task? What is your next social commitment relating to your research project and how do you need to prepare for it?
- Doing a research project requires **discipline**. You may need to be a little ruthless and forego some of your other interests and responsibilities for

DOI: 10.4324/9781003285137-19

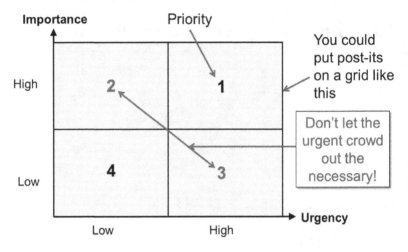

Figure 14.1 Task ranking by urgency and importance

a period of time, and learn to say "no" to some new demands on your time. Do you really need to be doing them now? Can someone else handle them?

- However, you still need to have a life outside of your research project. Make sure you **get sufficient rest**, **eat well**, and **don't withdraw socially**. You will perform better overall if you don't overdo things as you can easily wear yourself out.
- Try to maintain **accurate, organised records**, as these can help you when you need to refer back to what you have already done. One strategy is to keep a **research log** – a general book of notes accounting for your research project.

Getting started

One major challenge you may face is **how to get started** on a big new task, such as those covered in Chapter 16. Here are some tips for getting started and improving your productivity based on McMillan and Weyers (2011):

- Think about your **study environment**: Is it tidy? Is it too noisy? Could you change location and work more productively?
- Try to **avoid social distractions** – find a place and time where you can concentrate. This might mean switching off social media or your email inbox for a while.

Table 14.1 Example work breakdown structure

Task no.	Description	Effort	Who	Resources/comment
3.1	Develop pilot interview questions	6 hrs	Me	
3.2	Supervisor to check questionnaire	1 hr	Supervisor	Arrange meeting for 20th Feb
3.3	Arrange 3 interviews	2 hrs	Me	
3.4	Carry out 3 interviews	10 hrs	Me	Arrange payment
3.5	Analyse interview data	10 hrs	Me	Make comments in reflective journal
3.6	Send improved interview questions to supervisor	2 hrs	Me	

- Work in **short bursts** rather than pressuring yourself to achieve too much over a longer period.
- **Find a way to start**; even if it is not the task at the top of your list, do something relating to your research project that you feel comfortable with. Reject **displacement activities** – unrelated tasks which suddenly seem important because you are trying to face something difficult.
- Focus on **positives**, such as what you have already achieved, rather than what you haven't yet accomplished.
- Use a **non-linear approach to writing**; you can outline or draft some chapters whilst you refine others. You cannot hope to complete your chapters in linear order before starting the next one as you will surely run out of time.
- **Break down large tasks**; whilst Gantt charts are good for seeing the big picture, they lack the detail required to manage larger tasks. One way of managing this is through a **work breakdown structure**, which enables you to split a big task up and consider how much work is involved in each subtask, and by whom. An example is shown in Table 14.1.
- **Work alongside others**: whilst dissertation work is normally individual, there are ways that you can take advantage of other people's activities, such as your university friends or other people studying a research project. If you were to go to a study location together and take breaks at the same time, you could **set goals** and report back on your progress.
- **Ask for help**: if you get stuck, don't suffer on your own, but speak out to someone about it, such as your supervisor, a fellow student, or your dissertation coordinator. You can waste a lot of time and heartache by

keeping quiet when someone else might be able to assist you or at least point you in the right direction to find help.
- **Don't be a perfectionist**: some students find it hard to let go of their draft work because they are worried that it is not good enough and their supervisor might criticise them. It is your supervisor's job to give you feedback on your draft work and this is perhaps the most important thing that they do. They are not trying to criticise you – they are trying to help you to improve your work, and also to develop as a researcher and as an academic writer. This means that you need to have the courage to trust them with your draft work at the right moment. If you leave it too late you will not have enough time to make changes and you might already think your work is better than it actually is.

Finishing on time

According to Horn (2012) these are some common causes of delay in research projects:

- Problems accessing data or participants
- Illness
- Unavailability of resources
- Slow ethics approval, especially if your topic has been viewed as medium or high risk
- A difficult academic area – maybe the area you have chosen is relatively new and appropriate methods for undertaking research are not yet agreed
- A family or work crisis
- Delays in receiving feedback from your supervisor, or their feedback unexpectedly requires you to rewrite chapters or sections

The moral of all these common causes of delay is to **leave some contingency time** in your schedule. Failure to do so will make you feel stressed and mean that you will not do yourself justice as you will not be able to finish all the tasks involved in doing your dissertation to an adequate standard.

Here is some advice from some successful medical students (Rivera et al., 2005) on how to complete your dissertation on time:

- Start early
- Set aside adequate (protected) time each week
- Stick to your timeline
- Get the most out of your supervisory relationship

- Choose a topic that genuinely interests you
- Keep your project simple yet innovative

Stress management

Definition

Emotional, or human, stress is a concept derived from the concept of stress of physical objects. **Strain** means the amount of tension an object is placed under. **Stress** is the reaction of an object to being placed under strain.

Emotional stress occurs when you believe you can't cope with a problem or situation you perceive to be stressful (Lazarus and Cohen, 1984).

Causes

Here are some causes of stress relating to dissertations according to Fontana (1991):

- Insufficient support or leadership
- Long or unsociable hours
- Uncertainty or insecurity
- Unrealistically high expectations
- Inability to influence decisions (caused by a lack of assertiveness)
- Conflicts with your supervisor
- Poor communication
- Inability to finish a job

Stress and productivity

Students often feel stressed because they are **putting themselves under too much strain** as they are trying to achieve too much in the time they have allocated. With better planning and lower expectations of what you are trying to achieve over time, you can actually achieve more, especially in the long run.

If you feel you are working near to your limit, you need to **be kind to yourself, pull back** and **get some rest**. You cannot maintain maximum productivity over an extended period as your productivity will start to drop off. Once you get into a mindset of trying too hard you can do yourself physical harm such as exhaustion, ill health or even a breakdown, as well as not achieving as much.

Signs

Here are some possible signs of stress:

- Panic attacks
- Always feeling pressured and hurried
- Unable to take in new information, forgetful
- Being irritable, constantly in a bad mood
- Headaches, chest pain, and stomach problems
- Allergic reactions (e.g. skin conditions or asthma)
- Difficulty going to sleep
- Overeating or not eating properly
- New addictions or substance abuses
- Depression, constant sadness
- Being withdrawn

Please note that these are only indicators. They should not be trusted for self-diagnosis. On the other hand, you would not expect all these signs to be present in someone who was feeling stressed.

Tips on managing stress

- Try not to worry about things outside of your control
- Instead, try to identify the sources of stress in your life (known as **stressors**)
- **Talk to someone** about it (such as a friend, your supervisor, or a university counsellor)
- Start a **stress journal**: it may make it easier to write things down and reflect on how you are feeling, then start to deal with your situation
- Reflect on how you currently cope with stress: there are healthy and unhealthy ways – try not to start new unhealthy habits
- Do some exercise
- Have a good diet
- Find a relaxation technique that works for you

The 4 As of stress management

- **Accept**: When you can't change a situation, sometimes you just need to just accept it for what it is.
- **Avoid**: Plan ahead to rearrange your surroundings. For example, avoid taking on more than you can handle.
- **Alter**: Changing stressful situations may allow you to evade the stress all-together:

- Manage your time better
- Learn to be more assertive (see Chapter 15)

- **Adapt**: By anticipating the stressors in your life and making plans to adapt, you can save yourself a lot of aggravation:

  - Change your thinking
  - Change your feelings
  - Change your actions

Source: (Mayo Clinic Health System, 2022)

References

Coaching Positive Performance (2018) *17 Essential time management skills*. Available at: www.coachingpositiveperformance.com/17-essential-time-management-skills/.

Fontana, D. (1991) *Managing stress*. Hoboken, NJ: Wiley.

Horn, R. (2012) *Researching and writing dissertations: A complete guide for business and management students*. 2nd edn. London: CIPD.

Lazarus, R. and Cohen, J. (1984) *Stress, appraisal and coping*. 3rd edn. New York: Springer.

Mayo Clinic Health System (2022) *Need stress relief? Try the 4 A's*. Available at: www.mayoclinichealthsystem.org/hometown-health/speaking-of-health/the-4-as-of-stress-relief.

McMillan, K. and Weyers, J. (2011) *How to write dissertations and project reports*. 2nd edn. Upper Saddle River, NJ: Prentice Hall.

Rivera, J., Levine, R. and Wright, S. (2005) Completing a scholarly project during residency training: Perspectives of residents who have been successful. *Journal of General Internal Medicine*, 20(4), pp. 366–369.

15 Your supervisory relationship

Introduction

The dance metaphor

Your supervisory relationship is like performing a **dance** together (Derounian, 2011):

- The **content** of your writing is like dance steps
- Like dance steps, these need to be **executed correctly** (e.g. academic writing conventions, referencing, etc.)
- There needs to be an **overall message** which comes through in your writing (like choreography)
- Just as in dancing, there is a **personal relationship** between you and your supervisor which will affect the quality of the outcome
- Finally, just as there is another intangible "X-factor" in dancing (sometimes referred to as grace or poise), you need to **develop your "voice"** as an academic researcher and writer, demonstrating your confidence to communicate from your identity as a researcher

Supervisor styles

Supervisor approaches can be measured in terms of the level of structure and the level of support that they provide (Gatfield, 2005) – see Figure 15.1.

- A **pastoral** supervisor is high in support but low in structure.
- A **directorial** supervisor is low in support but high in structure.
- A **contractual** supervisor is high in both structure and support.
- The fourth supervisory style is called **laissez-faire** and refers to supervisors who are both low in structure and low in support. It has been written in grey text because it is viewed as being unprofessional.

DOI: 10.4324/9781003285137-20

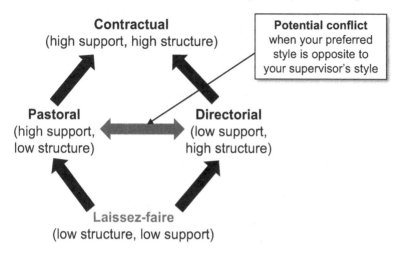

Figure 15.1 Dimensions of supervisory relationships
Source: Adapted from Gatfield (2005: 317)

The main point of the diagram is to explain that conflicts between students and supervisors can arise when a supervisor's preferred style is different from a student's preferred style.

Have correct expectations

Supervisors

You should expect your supervisor to:

- Be available for supervisory meetings to:
    - Assess your progress honestly
    - Provide you with verbal or written feedback
    - Agree on next steps for your research and help you set goals for your next meeting
- Advise you about reading and research, and help you to develop your ideas
- Help you to improve your research and writing ability
- Provide you with guidance and support throughout
- Review whether your research is manageable, suitably focused, and clearly prescribed

- Advise you on the preparation of your dissertation document (in terms of its structure, content, coherence and presentation)

However, you should **not** expect your supervisor to:

- Provide you with a "ready-made" research area
- Take responsibility for the progress of your dissertation
- Chase you to make an appointment with them
- Tell you in advance whether you will ultimately succeed, even if they approve of your current level of progress
- Respond to your emails immediately, out of hours, on annual leave or over the weekend
- Read your work at short notice or without an appointment
- Assist you with continual revisions of draft chapters
- Proofread or edit your work

Students

You should:

- Work conscientiously and independently, following your supervisor's guidance and feedback
- Be **proactive** by raising problems or difficulties with your supervisor early on
- Give your supervisor **sufficient notice** of requested meetings and send your draft work in advance
- Prepare for supervisory meetings having addressed prior action points with a clear agenda for the meeting
- Take notes during supervisions and send your supervisor a meeting summary soon after the meeting
- **Take responsibility for your own progress** by regularly reviewing your personal timeline (e.g. Gantt chart) to ensure your research is on track

Preparing for supervisions

- Focus on one main subject in each meeting.
- **Organise** your paperwork before, during and after the meeting.
- **Agree on actions and dates**. This is a form of public goal setting which will improve your outcomes (see Hayes et al., 1985).
- Let go of your draft at the right moment.

- Send your work enough time in advance for it still to be fresh in your mind but so that your supervisor has enough time to schedule producing helpful feedback. The ideal amount of time is usually about two to three working days.

After the meeting, you should send a **meeting summary sheet** to your supervisor via email within three days. This should include a summary of your discussion, agreed actions by both of you, and the agreed date of next meeting.

Learn to be assertive

Introduction

Many students fail to get what they need in supervisory relationships because they either stay quiet or they don't know how to ask without appearing rude or aggressive. Three approaches to relationships are shown in Figure 15.2.

Submissive or non-assertive people respect others, but they do not respect themselves. This means they do not get what they need. **Aggressive** people respect themselves, but they do not respect others. This means they may antagonise others and not get what they need. However, **assertive** people respect others and also respect themselves. This enables them to get what they need.

Figure 15.2 Approaches to relationships

Definition

Assertive people:

- Believe in:
    - Respecting others and themselves
    - Their values and rights
- Believe they have a right to:
    - Ask for what they want
    - Have an opinion
    - Make decisions
    - Make mistakes
    - Celebrate their successes
    - Change their mind
    - Be independent
    - Be respected
    - Refuse to do something (especially if they believe it would be unhelpful to their overall success)

Source (Smith, 2011)

Techniques

There are three main assertiveness techniques (Larsen and Jordan, 2017):

- **Broken record**: Find a suitable phrase to express yourself then repeat it without becoming emotional or justifying yourself further until you are listened to. For example, "This item is faulty. Under the sale of goods act I am entitled to my money back."
- **Empathy**: Express how you feel and that you are trying to understand how the other person feels. For example, "I understand you need help but I'm sorry I can't this time because . . .".
- Offer a **compromise** whilst maintaining your self-respect.

A combination of all three techniques is often best. The skill is to know which technique to use in which situation.

Tips for a successful relationship

How to nurture your supervisor

- Establish norms of how you will work together, such as the length and regularity of your meetings and how far in advance you should send your draft work

- **Incorporate your supervisor's recommendations into your revisions** (at least in part), otherwise they might become discouraged and not invest so much effort in giving you as detailed feedback another time
- Respect the time constraints of your supervisory meetings
- Take the initiative, but expect guidance
- Maintain contact.

Source: (Roberts, 2010)

Remember: it is **your** dissertation, not your supervisor's. They do not give you instructions, they give you advice. You have the right to say "no" and to make your own decisions. When you change your work based on their advice, you are not making corrections, you are learning to become a better researcher and writer, and putting it into practice.

Here is some further advice from Vitae (2022):

- Keep things in perspective – you are both human so either of you might have a bad day leading to a bad supervision meeting
- Any criticism your supervisor makes is almost always directed at your actions, not you personally (even when it seems personal)
- Be professional – accept criticism positively
- Ask for feedback – don't wait to be told what to do
- Show your enthusiasm
- Meet deadlines – set a good example

Dealing with criticism

- Try to take criticism of your work objectively, not personally – get over your emotional reaction then come back to it later so that you can evaluate it more objectively. Ask yourself:

  - Are the points made valid?
  - Can they help me to improve my work and become a better researcher or writer?

- Remember that your supervisor wants you to succeed.
- Also realise that having feedback is much better than not having it, even if it appears critical and negative.

If things become difficult

If you have tried the above techniques but none of them have worked and you feel you have a problem with your supervisor, this is what you should do:

- Contact your dissertation coordinator (informally at first):

- Ask them for advice.
- Ask them what the procedures are. This will help you to empower yourself, so you realise that you are not a victim, and that you have choices.

- **Keep a record of all issues**: by this stage you may be required to present factual evidence, such as email threads.
- **Seek a resolution**: there may be an existing procedure, such as a meeting between you, your supervisor, your programme leader and your student representative.
- There are four possible outcomes:

  - You realise that you are to blame and change.
  - Your supervisor accepts they were at fault, and they change.
  - You both realise that there is blame on both sides and you both change.
  - You are unable to reach an agreement. This is the point at which trust has broken down even though you have done your best to resolve the situation so this is when your dissertation coordinator should consider changing your supervisor.

As a dissertation coordinator of about 800 students per year, I never cease to be amazed at how many students ask me for a new supervisor for the smallest reason when they have not got anywhere near this stage. However, a few students genuinely reach this point and I do my best to intervene and help them.

References

Derounian, J. (2011) Shall we dance? The importance of staff – student relationships to undergraduate dissertation preparation. *Active Learning in Higher Education*, 12(2), pp. 91–100.

Gatfield, T. (2005) An investigation into PhD supervisory management styles: Development of a dynamic conceptual model and its management. *Journal of Higher Education Policy and Management*, 27(3), pp. 311–325.

Hayes, S. C., Rosenfarb, I., Wulfert, E., Munt, E. D., Korn, Z. and Zettle, R. D. (1985) Self-reinforcement effects: An artifact of social standard setting. *Journal of Applied Behavior Analysis*, 18(3), pp. 201–214.

Larsen, K. L. and Jordan, S. S. (2017) Assertiveness training. In: V. Zeigler-Hill and T. Shackelford, eds. *Encyclopedia of personality and individual differences*. New York: Springer Nature. https://doi.org/10.1007/978-3-319-28099-8_882-1.

Roberts, C. (2010) *The dissertation journey: A practical and comprehensive guide to planning, writing and defending your dissertation.* 2nd edn. London: SAGE.

Smith, M. J. (2011) *When I say no, I feel guilty*. New York: Bantam.

Vitae (2022) *Supervision and key relationships*. Available at: www.vitae.ac.uk/doing-research/doing-a-doctorate/starting-a-doctorate/supervision-and-key-relationships.

16 Next steps in your research

Introduction

Once you have submitted your proposal, you are moving from the conceptual phase to the **critical phase** of your research project (see Chapter 12). In this final chapter, we shall briefly explore the common tasks you will need to work on during your critical phase.

Responding to your proposal feedback

At some point, you should receive written feedback on your proposal. It is important that you get beyond your emotional reaction to your mark for coursework, or an accept/reject decision for proposals requiring formal approval.

Once you are in a more objective mindset you should read the feedback you were given in detail and see what you can learn about how to improve your work, your understanding of the research process and your ability as an academic writer.

The most important thing to focus on is to **get your topic right for your dissertation**. This is your main opportunity to receive detailed feedback on your topic and to decide whether it needs changing. You should be prepared to make changes and not be wedded to your proposal idea. However, as mentioned in Chapter 1, it is much better to **adapt an existing idea than start again from scratch**. From my experience, most proposal topic ideas are criticised for being **too broad in scope**. In addition, your supervisor may have thought that your plan for collecting and analysing data to investigate your chosen topic was not viable.

You will need to agree with your supervisor on a viable topic, then **rewrite your front matter** to make it consistent with your revised topic.

The other advice you have received in your feedback can help you with drafting the first few chapters of your dissertation. Make use of this good opportunity to improve your writing.

DOI: 10.4324/9781003285137-21

Drafting your introduction chapter

Your introduction chapter to your dissertation should be an extension of your introduction in your proposal. Many of the principles explained in Chapter 2 and Chapter 8 can be applied to it. You will need to go into more depth in your background and problem statement, but they should follow the same principles with unique distinct paragraph topics in your background being combined together and focused in your problem statement. Again, the combination of your background and your problem statement form your rationale for choosing your research topic.

The number of objectives and research questions might increase slightly, but their style is essentially the same as for your proposal. There may be some additional sections that you need to add to this chapter, such as your potential contribution.

Doing and drafting your full literature review

As for your dissertation introduction, your full literature review chapter should be an extension of your literature review in your proposal. Again, the style will be similar to that of a proposal literature review which was explained in Chapter 9.

You may have slightly more themes. They will no doubt be longer, and they may be divided into subsections, but you should not over-structure your review so that you leave plenty of opportunities for deeper, critical writing. You will need to obtain more references, but the ones you have already obtained for your proposal can form the basis of your research.

Your argument needs to be evidence-based and flow from one paragraph to the next. You should show critical thinking in your choice of supporting evidence and the length and style of your citations. The topics and points of your paragraphs need to be clear, and your paragraphs should be between 60 and 180 words long. You need to include theoretical perspectives and critical analysis. All these issues were discussed in Chapters 5, 6, 7 and 9.

Dissertation literature reviews tend to be about 25% of the total word-count. They should have a discussion at, or near, the end that is focused on your context and draws together the findings from the themes you have already presented. You might then finish your review with a conclusion in which you reappraise your research questions in the light of your findings.

Doing a full literature review is a complex task, so you may need to break it down with a work breakdown structure as explained in Chapter 14. You may also need several versions of your literature review as tasks on your Gantt chart, so it is clear when you plan to complete them and what feedback you are hoping to obtain from your supervisor.

Drafting your methodology/method chapter

As for your first two dissertation chapters, your methodology/method chapter should also be an extension of your methodology/method section from your proposal. It will probably be about 15–20% of your total wordcount. The main difference between the proposal and the dissertation versions is the tense and style: your dissertation version should be written in the **past tense** with a **more definite rationale style of argument** as the research will have been undertaken by the time this chapter is read.

As for your proposal, the methodology/method chapter should start with an introduction and be divided into sections which follow a logical order, as explained in Chapter 11. You are also advised to **include a conceptual framework** (see Chapter 10) as they are very helpful and there should be sufficient wordcount for this. However, you should be careful not to explain things to the reader that they already know, or add more sections which overlap in content and make the overall rationale and plan for carrying out your research project less clear.

Nevertheless, there may be sufficient wordcount for more discussion towards the end of some of your sections. This could address issues such as: your choices compared with viable alternatives, how these choices have been implemented, and potential limitations or issues you may face when carrying out the research. If you are carrying out quantitative analysis, you may have a longer discussion about validity, reliability and your hypotheses for statistical analysis. Again, please refer to Chapter 11 for an initial explanation.

There is no need for a conclusion at the end of this chapter.

Requesting ethics approval

Before you carry out primary data collection, most institutions require you to have first obtained ethics approval, so this will need to be completed during your critical phase.

Ethics approval works like an **insurance policy**: in the unlikely event that something goes wrong during your you have ethics approval then your institution is responsible; **if you do not have ethics approval then you are personally liable**.

The elements of the ethics approval process will be specific to your institution, and you should receive advice and training on this. For general information on the ethics process, please refer to www.ukri.org/councils/esrc/guidance-for-applicants/research-ethics-guidance/.

Designing your data collection instrument

If you are undertaking primary data collection during your research project, you will also need to design your data collection instrument during this phase. This should be based on your research questions and objectives and your conceptual framework.

You need to think carefully about what questions you wish to include here so that you can obtain the most useful data to answer your research questions and achieve your objectives. Try not to ask complicated questions. For questionnaires, data analysis is often based on a research design which involves a combination of question answers.

Your supervisor should give you feedback on your draft data collection instrument. You can also show some of your fellow students a draft version to see whether it makes sense to them.

For more information, please refer to the sources in the bibliography list below.

I hope you have found this book useful. I wish you every success with your proposal, your dissertation and your future career.

Bibliography

Alvesson, M. (2013) *Constructing research questions: Doing interesting research.* London: SAGE.

Fink, A. (2009) *How to conduct surveys: A step-by-step guide.* 4th edn. London: SAGE.

Frazer, L. and Lawley, M. (2000) *Questionnaire design and administration: A practical guide.* Chichester: Wiley.

Hammersley, M. and Atkinson, P. (2007) *Ethnography: Principles in practice.* 3rd edn. London: Routledge.

Oppenheim, A. N. (2000) *Questionnaire design, interviewing and attitude measurement.* New edn. London: Continuum.

Rea, L. M. and Parker, R. A. (2005) *Designing and conducting survey research: A comprehensive guide.* 4th edn. San Francisco: Wiley.

Rubin, H. and Rubin, I. (2005) *Qualitative interviewing: The art of hearing data.* 2nd edn. London: SAGE.

Index

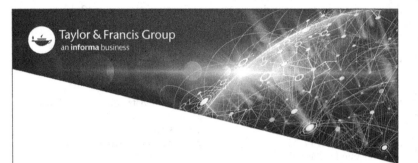

Printed in the United States
by Baker & Taylor Publisher Services